The Cambridge Manuals of Science and Literature

GREEK TRAGEDY

CAMBRIDGE UNIVERSITY PRESS

C. F. CLAY, Manager

LONDON : FETTER LANE, E.C.4

NEW YORK : THE MACMILLAN CO.
BOMBAY
CALCUTTA } MACMILLAN AND CO., LTD.
MADRAS
TORONTO : THE MACMILLAN CO.
OF CANADA, LTD.
TOKYO : MARUZEN-KABUSHIKI-KAISHA

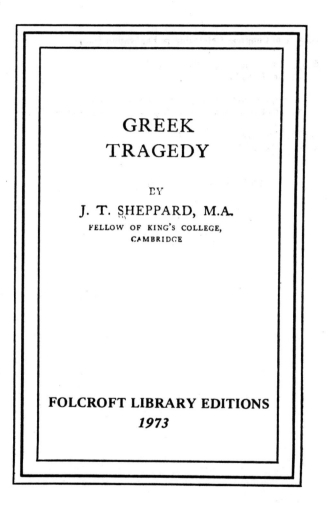

GREEK TRAGEDY

BY

J. T. SHEPPARD, M.A.

FELLOW OF KING'S COLLEGE,
CAMBRIDGE

FOLCROFT LIBRARY EDITIONS
1973

Library of Congress Cataloging in Publication Data

Sheppard, John Tresidder, 1881-
    Greek tragedy.

    Includes bibliographical references.
    1. Greek drama (tragedy)--History and criticism.
I. Title.
PA3132.S5 1973   882'.01'09   73-4010
ISBN 0-8414-7514-8

        Manufactured in the United States of America

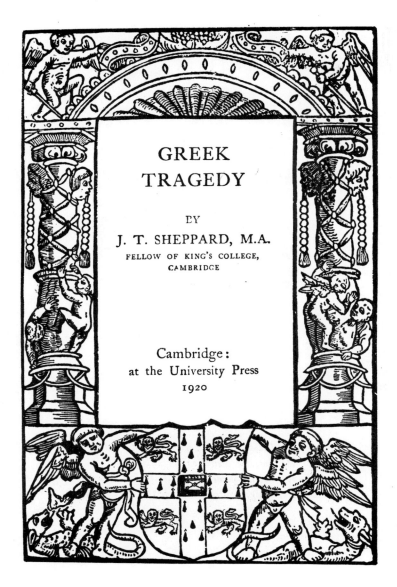

GREEK TRAGEDY

BY

J. T. SHEPPARD, M.A.

FELLOW OF KING'S COLLEGE,
CAMBRIDGE

Cambridge:
at the University Press
1920

First Edition 1911
Reprinted 1919, 1920

PREFACE

THIS book does not pretend to be a summary of known facts relating to Greek Tragedy. Nor is it, except incidentally, an essay in critical appreciation. Its aim is to help modern readers to enjoy Greek plays. For that reason stress has been laid on ideas and conventions which are not likely to be at first sight obvious to an English reader. That is why more space is given to Aeschylus than to either of his successors. That is also the explanation of the brief allusion which is made to some of the greatest of Greek tragedies. The *Oedipus Tyrannus*, for instance, depends for its effect upon qualities which are apparent, even in translation, to all readers who care for poetry and drama.

It may be added that this book will be of little use unless the reader will turn to the plays themselves, either in the original or at least in a translation. Finally, remarks which are made in regard to one play often apply with equal force to many others.

My indebtedness to the late Dr Walter Headlam will be apparent to all who know his work. I desire also to acknowledge my debt to the works of Professor U. von Wilamowitz-Moellendorf, Professor Verrall, Professor Ridgeway, Mr Austin Smyth, Mr A. C. Pearson, and other scholars too numerous to mention. For help in the preparation of this book I have to thank the editor, Dr Giles, Mr A. B. Cook, who helped me to choose the illustrations and kindly permitted me to reproduce fig. 2 (first published by him in the *Classical Review*, vol. IX., p. 373), Mr L. Whibley, who lent me the photograph from which fig. 4 is taken, Mr C. F. Taylor and Mr R. L. Sheppard.

J. T. SHEPPARD.

KING'S COLLEGE,
  CAMBRIDGE
    August 4, 1911.

AUTHOR'S NOTE

The study of Greek Tragedy has not stood still during the past eight years. Nor have I altogether failed, I hope, to learn from time and friendly criticism and fresh reading. Some of the opinions confidently expressed in this book now look doubtful, inadequate, or even false. But it has seemed best to leave the substance of the work unaltered, removing only a few of the more glaring errors, and adding something to the Bibliography. Had the book been written now, it would perhaps have done more justice to the art of Sophocles. It would certainly have been less favourable in its judgment of Verrall's general conception of Euripides, though not less indebted to the inspiration of his genius and of his noble intellectual enthusiasm. The best part of the book is the chapter on Aeschylus, and that is the part which follows most closely the teaching of Walter Headlam.

J. T. S.

King's College,
   Cambridge.
      May 11, 1919.

CONTENTS

CHAPTER I

ORIGINS

IN the *Persae* of Aeschylus the queen Atossa elicits from her councillors the astonishing fact that citizens of Athens "call no man master, and are called by no man slaves." That kind of sentiment was always welcome at Athens, and Tragedy, which expresses not only individual genius but also the collective feeling, was not slow to meet the demand. The three Tragedians, Aeschylus and Sophocles and Euripides, are poets of fifth-century democracy, and represent three phases of its life, the growth, the achievement, and the not less fruitful death-struggle. Aeschylus, who represents the age of effort and expansion, was born under the despots, and was a youth when, by the laws of Cleisthenes, the city won the form, if not the substance, of complete democracy. He fought at Marathon, which meant not only freedom from the barbarian, but also the assurance that the despotism would not be re-established, and he survived the constitutional changes which made Pericles supreme. The next thirty years are associated with the name of Pericles, who made effectual the power of the democracy and governed only because of his unrivalled personal ascendency. The steady but by no means effortless brilliancy of this generation is reflected in the poetry of Sophocles. When Pericles died, Athens had entered on the struggle in which, after tragic heroism, after suffering and triumph, sordid in turn and generous, she was stripped of power and humbled at the feet of Sparta. Euripides is the poet of this final age. Different as these three men are, they are all alike democratic. The willing subjects of laws which they themselves created and approved, Athenians and Athenian poets hated the name of tyrant, the symbol of lawless arbitrary power. Yet the arbitrary power of the Peisistratids had made democracy possible, and Tragedy, the poetry of the democracy, was nursed to greatness under the patronage of the sixth-century "tyrants."

Ultimately the power of a despot depended upon his popularity. That fact, not simply personal ambition, made Peisistratus build ships, encourage commerce, beautify the city, and by lavish hospitality attract poets and artists to his court. His support was to be found among the common people, relieved by his single rule from the oppression of the nobles. But the nobles who were concerned to discredit him had in religion a powerful weapon. The safety of the state depended on the due observance of religious rites; and the effective popular religion of Attica in the sixth century was connected with local Heroes rather than with the Olympian Gods. The local cults often associated with the grave of the Hero, who was a defender if propitiated, but if offended a dangerous enemy, were maintained and controlled by the heads of noble houses. To support a despot against the nobles of a clan was, therefore, to support an adventurer against the representatives of the local Hero. It was partly as an antidote that the despots encouraged the great Hellenic worship of Zeus and his interpreter Apollo. For this reason, among others, they assisted Delphi in the glorification of the great Hellenic Games. Peisistratus, for this reason, began the vast temple of Zeus, and gave the recitation of Homer a regular part in the religious ritual of the state: for the gods of Homer are Hellenic, not local. Finally, this is why he identified himself especially with the cult of Dionysus, a late arrival in Greece, a popular god, whose worship belonged to no special class of persons, and had, moreover, an element of enthusiasm admirably calculated to supplant devotion to the local cults.

To Dionysus Peisistratus built a new temple. In his honour he founded, or at any rate magnificently reconstituted, the festival known as the Great City Dionysia. At this festival in March 534 (or 535) B.C. the first tragic contest of the Athenian state took

1—2

place, and the victor, Thespis, must be honoured as reputed founder of the Attic drama. Already Thespis had performed at village festivals, but now for the first time his "Tragedy" was produced at the expense and for the honour of the city. As to the nature of his work and the influences which moulded Tragedy in the generation before Aeschylus, evidence is confusing, theories are numerous and too confidently maintained. Conjectures which seem to their authors mutually exclusive often appear to contain some elements of truth: for the Aeschylean drama is a complex work of art, developed under many artistic and religious impulses, not to be ascribed to any one exclusive "Origin." The task of these forgotten poets was to produce a performance worthy of a great new festival, impressive from a religious point of view and efficacious, and from the artistic point of view delightful. To these ends they must have devoted anything impressive in ritual, anything delightful in art which suited the general character of their composition.

The festival belonged to Dionysus of Eleutherae, a village on the northern border of Attica: and it is possible that this new Dionysus was introduced to the city by Peisistratus for his new festival. In any case, the coming of Dionysus Eleuthereus to Athens was commemorated every year by the procession in which the god was taken from his temple out along

the road to Eleutherae, brought back with pomp to
the place of the tragic performances and solemnly
seated to preside over the spectacle. Now a cult
epithet of this Dionysus was *Melanaigis*—the god

Fig. 1. Dionysus and Maenads.

with the black goat skin—a fact which has been
thought significant in view of the name *Tragoedia*,
or *goat-song*. Dionysus, it is argued, is the spirit of
life in all things, in trees and animals as well as in
the vine with which, in historical times, he is especially

associated. He is often represented as half man, half
tree (in fig. 1, for instance, where the god is a
draped pillar or tree-trunk with a human head, and
is decorated with grapes, ivy, honeycombs, and a
necklace of dried figs because he is the god of all
vegetation, not merely of the vine); and he might
be worshipped as an animal, particularly as a bull.
Further, in his cult the worshipper identifies himself

Fig. 2. A Boeotian Dionysiac Ritual.

with the god, becomes in fact by "enthusiasm" liter-
ally filled with the god. In other words the worshipper impersonates the god. Thus in fig. 2, the
dancer on the table (perhaps the most primitive form
of stage) is probably performing a rude dramatic
impersonation of the god, represented by the branch
on the left. His headdress is like that of Dionysus
in fig. 1. His wreath may be a prize. The Bacchants,

again, who tear and devour a living animal, do so in order that the life of the animal-god may fill them and make them potent. The singer of the dithyramb to Dionysus the Bull roars like a bull and becomes a bull himself. Similarly, it is suggested, the Satyrs with their horses' tails (cf. fig. 3) were originally worshippers of a Horse Dionysus, dressed up as horses in order to be sensitive to the god. Finally, the followers of the Goat Dionysus dressed themselves as goats.

The theory is obviously attractive : recent observations in Thrace and elsewhere have given it fresh allurement. Dionysus is still worshipped in his ancient haunts, though his worshippers are not aware of his identity. Mummers dressed in goat-skins, their faces covered with the skins, perform a dramatic ceremony in which a black-goat-man slays a white-goat-man, and the wife of the victim laments over her lord. Much of the ritual is obscene, and there is little doubt that the original intention was to promote fertility by reproducing in a magical performance the death and resurrection of the vegetation spirit. Some such ritual may well have belonged to Dionysus Melanaigis of Eleutherae. Can we then infer that the name of Tragedy, the mask, the lyrical lament, even the normal theme of tragedy—the *Pathos* (suffering, passion) of a god or hero—were already, in embryo, present in this ritual ?

The evidence for Dionysus the Goat is very slight: on such evidence it would be easy, as Dr Ridgeway says, "to turn the Olympian gods into a flock of goats." Athene, for instance, bears the *aigis*. The same scholar gives a more plausible account of the goat-skin worn by gods or worshippers, by pointing out that a goat-skin is the primitive peasant's dress, and that ritual is invariably conservative about costume. Still it is possible to under-rate the Dionysiac element in the making of drama. A ritual such as has been described has elements both of seriousness and of obscenity. The latter element found its affinity in the Satyric drama, said to have been introduced from the Peloponnese some years after the victory of Thespis. Throughout the fifth century tragic poets were expected to conclude their series of three tragedies with a Satyr play, lighter in tone, commonly performed by a chorus of the rustic, half-bestial attendants of Dionysus. This type of drama does not here concern us, for it is not Tragedy. Readers who care to pursue the enquiry into this direct offspring of the Dionysiac worship may be referred to Shelley's translation of the *Cyclops*.

The serious element (appropriate to such a conception of Dionysus as is seen in fig. 3) may well have been developed by poets who desired to add splendour to the festival. Already the worship of Dionysus had found artistic expression in the dithyramb. This hymn (perhaps originally a rustic improvisation to the Bull Dionysus) had been elaborated into a work of art by Arion of Lesbos (the home

Fig. 3. Dionysus with Satyrs.

of music) at the court of another tyrant, Corinth. Competitions in the singing and dancing of dithyrambs between choirs of men and boys were a regular

part of the Dionysiac festival at Athens.   They were
distinct from the tragic contests, but no doubt influenced the musical part of Tragedy.   The number of
performers was, for instance, fixed by Arion at fifty;
and it is quite likely that the Suppliants of Aeschylus
were actually fifty in number.   In any case the Dorian
choral lyric must have been the obvious model for
a poet who desired to give artistic form to any public
worship, and of all forms of lyric the dithyramb was
most likely to influence the poet who was honouring
Dionysus.   The subject, however, might be entirely
unconnected with the god.   Tradition says that the
people objected to the introduction of alien myths,
and cried, "Nothing to do with Dionysus."   It may
have been so.   But the change is not without pre-
cedent.   When an epic reciter celebrated a god at
his own festival, he would often dismiss the god in
a few lines or a perfunctory formula and pass at
once to some heroic story more interesting to his
audience.   It is not known how soon the dithyramb
was used for other than Dionysiac themes, but
Simonides of Ceos (born about 556 B.C.) composed
one in honour of a Hero, Memnon, son of the
Morning.   It is not known, again, how far the tendency of human beings to be dramatic had affected
choral lyric at this time.   The chorus may already
have broken into groups who addressed each
other in a lyrical dialogue : the leader may have

sometimes addressed them in a narrative interlude, or even assumed the character of a god or hero or messenger, purporting to give his narrative as a piece of news. The quaint processional in which Alcman (about 640—600 B.C.) led the Spartan maidens shows this tendency at work. Finally, it is generally held that the dialect of the tragic chorus is a conventional modification of the already conventional dialect of the Dorian choral lyric.

But perhaps the most important contribution to the new art form came after all from the local cults to which Peisistratus appears to have been devising an antidote. The worshippers of the hero probably danced about his tomb, reminded him of his mighty deeds, taunted him to stir him to activity, sometimes actually dressed up and impersonated him that their invocation might be more effectual. Such performances certainly resemble, and may have suggested, scenes like the invocation of Agamemnon in the *Choephoroe*, and the raising of the ghost of Dareius in the *Persae*. In many plays the altar in the centre of the dancing-place is for dramatic purposes regarded as the funeral mound of a hero-king. Such facts as these, viewed in the light of many parallels from the history of ancient drama all the world over, seem to point, as Professor Ridgeway has said, to an incorporation of the ancient hero-worship (perhaps already dramatic) into the new Dionysiac festival of Peisistratus.

Now the Homeric epic was the noblest existing glorification of the deeds and suffering of heroes. Peisistratus was the zealous propagator of the epic, for the heroes were there treated as Hellenic, not local, as great men, not as potentates of the grave. Naturally the new art found inspiration in the themes and an example in the tone of Homer. It must be remembered that by Homer in this connection is meant the great body of poetry known as the Epic Cycle, including the tale of Troy with all its ramifications, the legends of Thebes and the house of Laius, and many other myths. The recitation of the epic must have influenced the speeches of the god or hero or messenger who provided spoken interludes to song and dance : the metre adopted for these interludes was indeed the trochaic, later the iambic, but the tone became that of the lofty rhetoric of Homer.

Such and indeed more numerous than these were the elements which contributed to the making of the early Tragedy. The mimetic ritual of Dionysus, the worship of the Hero at his grave, the dithyramb or choral hymn to Dionysus, other forms of the choral lyric, and the narrative of the Homeric reciter, must all alike have guided the artists who, under the patronage of the despots, created primitive tragedy.

CHAPTER II

SOME GENERAL CHARACTERISTICS

It is said that before Aeschylus *Tragedy* was the song and dance of a chorus, relieved by interludes in which a single actor assumed a character, delivered a speech, or conversed with the leader of the chorus. Aeschylus is said to have created *drama* by the introduction of a second actor. However that may be, Tragedy in his hands was still at first a series of connected lyrics, sung by a chorus, and relieved by interludes of speech. The second actor made it possible for these interludes to present an independent action; and since action is more vivid than choral song the dramatic element was certain to conquer the lyrical. Yet throughout its history Greek Tragedy bears marks of its origin. It is never completely dramatic, nor can it ever be completely understood if it is judged by standards of modern dramatic criticism.

The modern theatre must be forgotten. We must not imagine ourselves sitting in darkness, while, on the stage, a piece of life is presented, framed like

a picture by the proscenium, but in appearance as
like reality as can be contrived. The Greek performance was in the open air : actors and spectators
and chorus were all in the same broad daylight. The
audience sat in a great half-circle of benches on the
slope of a hill. The centre of interest was not the
stage at all (at least not before the *Oresteia*), but
a circular dancing-floor (see fig. 4). Beyond this floor,
on the side away from the spectators, was a wooden
building, to which the performers could retire to
change their costume. At first this building was
simply a changing-room, not part of the imagined
scene. Sophocles (while Aeschylus was still exhibiting,
probably before the *Oresteia*, 458 B.C.) brought the
background into the action, and had it painted.
Even so we are far from modern scene-painting. It
is improbable that the appearance of the painted
building was changed for different plays : in general
the words of the drama would sufficiently indicate
whether it represented a temple or a palace. Further
indications may have been given by the showing of
conventional symbols or tokens. Contemporary vase-
paintings give a hint of the possible nature of such
devices : in these a temple of Apollo is suggested
by a laurel and a tripod, the sea by a dolphin (cf.
fig. 7, p. 69) and wavy lines, a mountainous country
by a goat and a rock. But the words alone are
generally enough. Action supposed to pass within

the building was displayed by an astonishing convention. Whether a platform was wheeled out through the central door, or (as is sometimes asserted) a part of the painted wall turned on a hinge and brought

Fig. 4. Theatre at Epidaurus showing circular dancing-place and auditorium.

out with it a platform, in any case the group or tableau thus presented, though it *indicated* that an interior was supposed to be seen, actually *represented* nothing like the inside of a building. I do not know what was the appearance of the *machine* on which gods were hoisted, and supposed to be flying in the air ; the effect, in broad daylight, can hardly have been realistic.

All this must be remembered when we interpret the plays. They are not representations realistic and of real events. "What child is there," wrote Sidney, "that cometh to a play, and seeing Thebes written in great letters upon an old door, doth believe that it is Thebes ? " As on the Elizabethan stage, the background is indicated, not expressed : as in the contemporary painting of Polygnotus, attention is concentrated on the human actor.

But the actors themselves presented no realistic picture. Whether they normally stood on a raised platform is disputed : if, as I think, there was a platform, it was probably long and narrow, ill adapted for realistic grouping. Moreover, there stood in the foreground a company of twelve or fifteen persons, whose grouping with the actors may have been beautiful, but must in itself have forbidden realism. Further, the actors wore masks (fig. 5), a religious convention which not even Euripides dared to abandon. Words must have been used where nowadays the actor's face would be enough : one great aid to the portrayal of individual character was lost ; in the play, as on the mask, a fixed type of character, a dominant emotion was likely to be presented : above all the lack of facial change was

Fig. 5. Tragic actors with masks. The actor on the left of the picture is looking in a mirror, the second has a mask (and a tambourine?), the third a mask. The youth on the couch is Dionysus, here represented, by a variation of a common art-type, as a hero receiving a procession of worshippers.

a hindrance to the modern kind of realistic illusion. Whether the actor was also padded and wore high buskins is less clear: but there is little doubt that the movements were stately rather than active, the grouping statuesque, the gesture ("dancing with the hands," they called it) rhythmical. What was demanded in an actor was a fine presence and a good voice. His duty was to speak his lines clearly, musically, and with appropriate conventional gesture. On the poetry, therefore, not on the scenery or the acting, must have depended the illusion, if illusion there was.

The play itself will often be found to lack the qualities for which a modern spectator looks. The speeches, for example, do not always seem appropriate. What seems appropriate in a play is not, of course, what would be natural in real life: but we expect at least an illusion of naturalness. Of our three dramatists, Sophocles alone appears consistently to have aimed at this effect. Aeschylus permits any imaginative utterance which contributes to the poetical elaboration of his theme, Euripides any thoughts which are naturally suggested by the situation. Rhetoric may take the place of character-drawing; patriotic or religious sentiment may be stirred by sentences dramatically indefensible. We shall go astray if we are exasperated by such anomalies: still more dangerous is it by violence or subtlety to force them into dramatic significance.

Similarly in the plot we are liable to insist upon a natural or logical sequence of events : modern ideas of causality make some of us peculiarly sensitive here. Dramatic logic again is not the logic of real life : but in Greek drama Sophocles alone maintained the illusion of a natural sequence of events. Even he was using a different art from that of modern stage-craft, for the audience knew the outline of his story before the play began. That meant not only absence of the delightful conjecture "How it will all end," but also that an event was plausible, however illogical, however inconsistent with what has gone before, simply because it was in the story. Those who are familiar with the kind of events which occur in a melodrama, are not surprised, do not ask, "Is it physically possible?" when British troops spring up from nowhere in the nick of time : still less need a Greek dramatist trouble about plausibility, since the audience knew not only the kind of event, but actually the particular event which was to happen.

It is clear that some effort of imagination is needed if we are to get all the possible pleasure from the reading of these dramas. But the imagination must not be of realistic scenery, of vivid action, of subtle implications in the plot. An ancient

2—2

spectator would probably find a bad modern play quite admirable in these respects : but he would miss other things which we do not demand, essential parts of his own drama, which we shall not notice unless we look for them.

In the first place the drama was a religious function and a great state festival. Not that the audience felt as if it was in church. A more helpful analogy is the feeling of devout spectators at the *Festa* of some popular saint. Such an audience is bent on enjoyment ; it is intensely alive and critical. But a solemnity from time to time supervenes, and the performance, if it is to be approved, must not only give pleasure, but also be felt worthy of a great occasion, likely to satisfy divine as well as human spectators. In the Dionysiac theatre there sat to watch the play not only magistrates and priests and eminent foreigners, but also Dionysus himself.

The audience was not a chance collection of persons, seeking relaxation after a day's work, but the free population of Athens (perhaps, though not certainly, women as well as men), keeping holiday. In the time with which we are most concerned there were also representatives of subject cities, bearers of tribute to Athene's treasury, sharers, in return, of the glory of her city. The festival included a procession, sacrifices on behalf of the state, contests in song and dance by chosen choirs of men and boys.

The time of year was early spring, when the earth,
like Dionysus, puts off the sleep of winter, and the
sea-ways are again open for the ships.   For this
festival Pindar sang:

> Look favourably on our dance, Olympians: shed over it the
> beauty of song, ye gods, who visit in your holy Athens the altar
> that stands in her midst, wreathed with incense, thronged with
> worshippers, and her famous market-place, gloriously adorned.
> Accept our garlands violet-entwined, our drink-offerings of the
> gifts of spring, and look favourably on me, the poet, who am sent
> by Zeus with a glittering gift of song.   Come, singers, praise the
> Ivy-garlanded, the god whom men call Bromios, Dionysus of the
> thunderous shout.   The Highest fathered him whom I am come
> to praise, and his mother was a woman of my own Thebes.   Plain
> token is it, noted of the god himself, that the festival is due,
> when the chamber of the red-robed Hours is opened and odorous
> plants wake to the fragrant spring.   Then, we scatter on undying
> Earth the violet, like lovely tresses, and twine roses in our hair:
> then sounds the voice of song, the flute keeps time, and dancing
> choirs resound the praise of Semele (*Fragment* 75, Bergk).

We must add the dust and turmoil and human
pettiness of a highly excitable people : the poet,
of course, idealises.   But when we think of the
seventeen thousand human beings who at such a
season, at such a festival, crowded the wooden
benches of the open-air theatre, we realise how pale
a shadow of Greek Tragedy we possess.

But imagination has still work to do.   The dance
and music are lost : yet they were an essential part
of the performance.   To us the lyrics often seem to

interrupt the drama. However that may be in
Euripides, in Sophocles they often give us clues
which may prevent complete misunderstanding of
his spirit : in Aeschylus each drama should be treated
as a single poem, and the lyrics are as important as
the dialogue.   .

The relation between chorus and action will be
made clear if we remember what was the history
of the legends before they fell into the hands of
Athenian dramatists. The poets who turned the
ancient myths into artistic epic, had, consciously
or unconsciously, impressed upon the stories their
own view of life. Their object was to tell a good
story, but the story told was, naturally, more moral,
more suited to a comparatively civilised audience,
than the crude legends on which it was based. This
poetry was brought by travelling minstrels from
Ionia, and introduced to noble houses in Greece
proper ; but the impulse to imaginative creation was
here for a time suspended. An age of reflection and
moralising ensued. Some poets occupied themselves
in arranging the legends, filling up gaps, systema-
tising genealogies, a work of which the *Theogony* of
Hesiod may serve as an example. At the same time
a new field was opened by the working into literary
shape of popular proverbial morality. When poetry
revived, the epic stories and the moral proverbs
were combined in the choral lyric. The deeds of

gods and heroes were now used as crystallised
morality, the maxims as generalisations on the facts
of the myths.   This tendency, which we can most
conveniently observe in Pindar (a contemporary of
Aeschylus), was at work before his time.   Add that
in Greece the heroes were not simply as in Ionia
great men of the past, but worshipful and potent
daimones in the grave: add too that a wave of
mystical religion swept over Greece in the sixth
century, accompanied by a new demand for righteousness not only in man but also in the objects of his
worship: remember, finally, that Ionian speculations,
at first physical, had by the time of the birth of
Tragedy produced in individual thinkers—Xeno-
phanes, for instance—a conscious demand for morality
in gods and heroes, and for a unity and moral government behind the world.   All this has its bearing on
Tragedy: for Tragedy regards the particular story
as a vivid illustration of the working of things in
general, and the general maxim as the theoretical
basis, the inner meaning of the myth.   Thus the
chorus shows the universal significance which makes
the dramatic tableau important, and the drama
vivifies the general reflection of the chorus.   The
speeches of Thucydides will illustrate the way in
which Greek artists give universal significance to
particular events.

So much for the lyrics in general: the music and

the dance must have given the audience a feeling of
their importance and a pleasure in them which
imagination can only dimly revive. In the ideal
Greek lyrical poetry, words and song and dance are
one. Each is bound up with, each interprets the
other two. Though much is obscure in the matter
of Greek music and dancing, this at least is certain,
that they were essentially *imitative* : that is to say,
particular scales and rhythms, particular kinds of
movement and grouping were appropriate to certain
definite sorts of idea and emotion. Doubtless the
appropriateness was often conventional, and would
not be intelligible to us if we could witness a performance, but the fact that they were appropriate
is established. For the music metre is our guide.
A modern libretto, of course, would be a very bad
guide to the musical rhythm : but Greek poetry is
different. Orchestral music was unknown ; harmony
was practically non-existent. A Tragic ode was sung in
unison, to the accompaniment of a flute ; words were
closely wedded to tune ; one syllable normally represents one note. The rhythm of the words, therefore, if
we can feel it, may help us to imagine the musical
effects. And the only way to feel it is to read with
the ear attentive, remembering the analogy of music.
It is fatal, as Dr Headlam said, to start by splitting
poetry into feet. Greek poetry is indeed based upon
longs and shorts, not, as is English poetry, mainly

upon accent or stress : but quantity has its effect
in English, and in Greek some short syllables are
stressed, some long ones are not. In English and
Greek and music, it is not the foot or bar which
matters, but the rhythmical phrase.

An ode is made up of stanzas, which are arranged
in pairs, or groups of three. The two which make
the pair correspond exactly, or almost exactly, in
longs and shorts : their effect is made subtly different by the nature of language and the division of
the words : but their scansion is syllable for syllable
practically identical. In a group of three stanzas,
the first two correspond, and the third is a new
treatment of rhythms already heard or suggested in
the first pair. Now each stanza is a rhythmical movement built up, like a piece of music, out of a number
of phrases. The rhythmical character of the whole
depends on the character of its phrases. Sometimes
these are few and the treatment is simple : sometimes phrases of different kinds are combined with
subtlety and elaboration. All that is necessary is
to learn a few simple rhythmical phrases which were
familiar to the audience and their associations of
meaning (see Appendix, p. 156) ; and then to read
the whole stanza aloud, as a continuous piece of
rhythm, observing the natural emphasis of the sentence (which tends in Greek to be strong at the
beginning and to weaken as the sentence proceeds),

and noticing how the simple phrases are combined, modified and elaborated. If the musical treatment seems curiously free, we must remember that we are dealing with the offspring of extemporised folk-singing, naturally free in composition. The effect is often that of improvisation, but the more we read the more we shall feel that the phrasing was deliberate and artistic.

As to the melody we know little, but it is clear that the so-called " Modes," were different methods of composition expressive of different kinds of feeling, the Dorian strenuous, solemn and virtuous, the Aeolian spirited, the Lydian luxuriant in joy or grief, oriental. Probably the differences were partly the result of different scales, i.e. scales in which the intervals observed were different. In folk music such freedom in the arrangement of the scales is common.

Finally, the dance itself was expected to be expressive of ideas.

The words therefore are only part of the poem, and were made more, not less, intelligible by the dance and song. The effect might to us seem thin, but there is abundant evidence that the Greeks were peculiarly responsive to subtleties of rhythm and tune. The best commentary on the importance attached to music as potent to affect not simply emotion but morality, is Plato's banishment of certain kinds of music from his ideal Republic.

We can now better understand how the absence of realism and the lack of originality in subject-matter were tolerated. The drama was not a realistic but a poetic "imitation" of life. The interest was not in the unfolding of an unknown sequence of events, but in fresh treatment of familiar matter. Familiar legends, rich in religious and patriotic associations, were made vivid by dramatic representation, and invested with new value by the spectacle, the language, the music, the dance; in all these departments the poet took old material, modified it, worked it into fresh forms, impressed upon it his own personality, and so created something new. It is not a case of Dryden's *chapon bouillé*; Aeschylus, Sophocles and Euripides could create three, and more than three, original works from the same old story " worn so threadbare by the pens of all the epic poets, and even by tradition itself of the talkative Greeklings, that before it came upon the stage it was already known to all the audience : and the people, as soon as they heard the name of Oedipus, knew as well as the poet, that he had killed his father by a mistake, and committed incest with his mother, before the play; that they were now to hear of a great plague, an oracle and the ghost of Laius : so that they sat with a yawning kind of expectation, till he was to come with his eyes pulled out, and speak a hundred or two verses

in a tragic tone, in complaint of his misfortune."
All that is true, except the "yawning kind of expectation," nor must we forget that the poets were
creating new poetry out of old material when we
turn, as it is high time to turn, to the concrete
examples of this ancient tragic art.

CHAPTER III

The Supplices

At the tragic competition each poet produced four plays. Aeschylus usually made his four a connected whole, so that the first three were like three acts of one great drama, and the fourth (the Satyric play) was a lighter epilogue, loosely connected with what had gone before. The *Oresteia* is the only surviving trilogy, and the other plays (except perhaps the *Persae*) are parts of larger works. Each has a certain unity, but for full understanding they require the illumination which could only come from knowledge of the whole.

The *Suppliant Women* is probably the first play of a trilogy, whose story was apparently treated as follows. In the first part (our play) the fifty daughters of Danaus fled from their home in Egypt to escape marriage with their cousins, the sons of Aegyptus. They took refuge at Argos, which espoused their

cause. In the second part (probably through the
defeat of the Argives), the women had fallen into
the hands of their cousins and the detestable marriage had been consummated : but, at the command
of their father, all the brides save one, Hypermestra,

Una de multis face nuptiali digna...,

killed their husbands. In the third and last play
the bride who cared more for the marriage tie than
for her father's will, was tried for disobedience and
acquitted through the intervention of Aphrodite
herself. Thus the heroine of the whole is Hypermestra, who in the *Suppliant Women* is in no way
distinguished from the rest of the chorus. Her trial
is the culmination of the performance, and our play
could not be understood without reference to her
fate. It is important to observe that the reason for
her disobedience was probably not a romantic passion
for her husband, but the desire of offspring. Hypermestra is here celebrated as a heroic ancestress of
Argive kings. The theme of the whole trilogy is the
mysterious will of Zeus, who produces good out of
apparent evil, and is working through the suffering
of the suppliants, through the horror of the murder
at night and the distraction between the duties of
daughter and wife, to the prosperity of a noble city.
The prayers of the suppliants for Argos are apparently
rejected in the second part : in the third part the

acquittal of Hypermestra is the token that, in an
• unexpected way, through her descendants, the city
is, after all, to be blessed.

Though the heroine is simply one of the fifty in
the first part, we are prepared for the subsequent
development by a division in the chorus. In the
first ode and in the processional which concludes one
play, some of the women speak as if it were certain
that the will of Zeus is against the marriage, but the
rest reply in terms which hint that even this marriage
may be part of his inscrutable plan.

The ways of Zeus, indeed, wind beyond their dis-
cerning. For Aeschylus, not only the punishment
but also the sin of the sons of Aegyptus was part of
the World's harmonious plan: and the proof of it
was modern Argos, the friend of Athens, sprung from
Hypermestra and the husband she spared. That is
why the maidens dispute among themselves in the
first ode; why, in the final procession, when Artemis
the virgin has been invoked against the marriage,
there is also a tribute to Aphrodite, mother of Persuasion and of Desire; and why, when some of the
maidens cry out wildly against the threatened fate,
others, more prudent, again declare that the mind of
Zeus is unfathomable and bid their sisters be moderate
in their prayer.

For this drama, the earliest we possess, no stage
should be imagined, but simply the circular dancing-

floor, and in the midst of it a mound or altar, adorned with images (or symbols) of the gods who guard the• city.   The dancing-floor, then, vaguely stands for the market-place of Argos, whither there marches a procession of fifty maidens, white-robed, dark-complexioned, carrying suppliant branches.   Their first words sound the key-note of the whole performance:

> Zeus the Suppliant look graciously on our company, on us who took ship and launched from the fine-sanded mouths of Nile! For the land we have left is His, the land whose pastures march with Syria. No outlawry is this, decreed by public vote for bloodshed, but an exile chosen in abhorrence of a sinful wedlock—with near kindred—with the folly-prating sons of Aegyptus.

At this point a question arises which, I believe, did not occur to most of the audience, though Aeschylus, who was interested in the early history of Hellas, may have thought of it.   Why was this marriage of first cousins sinful?   How was it that the Danaids thought the dangers of exile preferable? Not because of Athenian custom, for at Athens cousins married freely enough: nor because of Egyptian scruples, for in Egypt the kings married not only their cousins but their sisters, and did it on religious grounds.   The answer probably lies in the suggestion that the story represents the transition from matriarchy, under which property descends in the female line, to patriarchy, under which inheritance is by the male.   The matriarchal heiress takes a husband outside her clan, and the property goes with her : marriage with her own kin is taboo. As life becomes settled, property increases, and the males object to its alienation : so they insist on marrying the women of their clan. That may well be the origin of the story, and in the conventional treatment there may be hints of its origin. But if matriarchy ever prevailed in Athens, it would still be dangerous to assume that the struggle between matriarchy and patriarchy continued or was even remembered so late as the fifth century. Nor is there evidence apart from this play that marriage of cousins was at the date of its production questionable conduct.

Persons in the audience, however, who had married their cousins, may perfectly well have sympathised with the Suppliants for two reasons. The first is that "it was all in the story," and it requires considerable circumspection to apply our own morality to a traditional religious story. How many people to-day seriously suppose that Uzzah's kindly impertinence merited death, or David's census a devastating plague ? Yet the sins of Uzzah and of David would make excellent dramatic incidents, and it would be an unimaginative mind which did not thrill at the recital, morality or no morality, of these fine examples of human presumption and divine wrath. Similarly with the Suppliants, "it is all in the story." But

there is another reason. Aeschylus, while he keeps
the traditional tag, "marriage with kindred, wicked,
impious," lays stress on the fact that the kinsmen
are insolent and force the marriage on unwilling
daughters •of an unwilling father. If it is really a
plain case of matriarchy against patriarchy, it is
strange that the father of the maidens is so vague
in his protestations. "Take sanctuary," he bids them,
"like a flock of doves, fearful of hawks like-plum-
aged—the kinsmen, your enemies, who pollute the
race. Shall bird eat bird and be pure?" After all
it is not a question of bird eating bird, but of
marriage : the word *phagoi* shows that it is the
violence of the men that is really detestable. And
Danaus proceeds : "can bird eat bird and be pure?
And how should one be pure that takes *from an
unwilling father an unwilling bride?*"

So then, though the origin of the story is interesting,
what mattered for the audience was the fact that the
suitors were violent, barbarian, not Greek, not *aidoioi*
in their behaviour. As they were violently sinful in
their wooing, so, by the regular Aeschylean justice,
violence slew them on their wedding night.

Return now to the opening words : "Zeus look
graciously upon us, Zeus the Suppliant!" The word
used means not "the god of suppliants," but "the
Suppliant"; and this may serve as peg for a remark
important in its bearing on the meaning of the

drama. A worshipper is regarded as affecting a god by his prayer : he assumes the character of the god in order to influence him : he actually makes the god assume the character of the worshipper in order to be more easily influenced. That is why Zeus is called the Suppliant here. But the principle is important in another way. The chorus throughout the play draw a parallel, not simply poetical, between their fate and that of Io. In fact they assume the character of Io in order to claim from Zeus the blessing which, after suffering, he conferred on Io ; to claim from Argos, no doubt, the help which is due to the off-spring of Argive Io ; but also to claim from Zeus the help which is due to the representatives of Zeus-loved Io. That is what makes the drama a drama at all : without the effectual assimilation of the maidens to Io the poem is, what it has often been thought to be, a collection of beautiful and slightly relevant lyrics and one dramatic scene.

The lyrics, then, about Io, had a dramatic signifi-cance, not merely a poetic : the audience was familiar with her story. To illustrate the importance of know-ing the stories before we judge the drama, I have used her name without explaining who she was.

A princess, and the priestess of Hera in Argos, she was loved by Zeus : Hera was jealous, transformed the maiden into a cow and set the keen-eyed Argus to watch her and prevent the amorous approach of

Zeus : Hermes, the messenger of Zeus, slew Argus, but Hera sent a gad-fly to torment the "horned maiden" and to drive her in a wretched flight over sea and land : her wanderings ended in Egypt, where Zeus restored her to human shape, had union with her and begat a divine son, Epaphus. The story is told in the *Prometheus* of Aeschylus. Now Io, like the daughters of Danaus, was an exile : like them, she had a marriage forced upon her ; like them, she suffered. Her sufferings were caused by Zeus, who delivered her *by his divine touch,* and *by the in-breathing of his divine spirit* : and she bore him a son, Epaphus, named of the touch of Zeus, the ancestor of the daughters of Danaus. To Argos the suppliants come, because Argos is the land of Io. The drama of the first scene is this—that Zeus himself is being compelled by the self-identification of the suppliants with Io to accept them as peculiarly his own.

This also is the religious idea of the first great ode ; it is the constraining of Zeus to aid his own offspring. But the comparison with Io is used throughout the play as a poetic theme full of suggestion. The mystic breath of Zeus delivered Io : that is why the chorus pray that they may meet not simply *aidôs* (the reverence due to suppliants), but "a breathing of reverence from the land." And again the divine *Epipnoia* suggests the poetical use of breathings.

winds, favourable winds for the suppliants (*Ourios Zeus*), and storms for the sons of Aegyptus. The divine Touch is also used as a recurrent theme. Like our own rite of consecration, this touching by the god is derived from the laying on of hands by a physician: so throughout we have allusion to disease and healing: "Zeus is the only remedy." To this strain of allusion we shall presently recur.

Meanwhile we may return to the drama. Having secured Zeus as their ally, the suppliants perform a litany to the gods of Argos, every sentence of which increases the unseen forces on their side. Their father's exhortation to a modest bearing "such as befits strangers" is couched in sententious terms, characteristic of the anxious, rather self-important old man: but the modesty displayed is also effectual for good.

Divine aid thus achieved, the time has come for human aid to be secured. A chariot and soldiers are seen approaching, and the king Pelasgus appears. His authority is made obvious by the pomp of his arrival: but the chorus enquire whether he is to be addressed as king or commoner simply in order that he may make a speech. "I am the son of Palaechthon the earthborn, Pelasgus, ruler of this land: and the people that reaps the fruit of it is named *Pelasgian* after me their king." He proceeds to speak of the extent of the city's territory, and concludes with a

piece of ancient history which at first sight looks
undramatic and otiose. "This plain of the Apian
land itself has long borne its name in honour of a
mediciner of old : from Naupactus on the further
shore came Apis, leech and seer, son of Apollo, and
purged this land of deadly monsters" (visitations of
the wrath of the Chthonic powers aroused by polluting
blood). "For these did Apis by surgery and spell
work cures to satisfaction, and by way of meed won
from the land of Argos mention in her prayers." (See
Dr Headlam's translation, from which I quote.)

What is the point of all this ? In the first place
the name Pelasgian stood for the earliest inhabitants of
Greece, possessors of the land before Achaean and
Dorian invaders swept down from the North : the
name was sure to have its effect on Athenian ears,
since it was the pride of Athenians that they were
themselves autochthonous and had dwelt in Attica
without shock or disturbance from time immemorial.
Pelasgus, then, is the type of the most ancient Argive,
addressing suppliants among whom, though he does
not know it, stands one who is to be the ancestress of
a new Argos. From such a personage, speaking to
such suppliants, the allusion to Apis, "leech and seer,"
who came across the strait to civilise the ancient realm,
is doubly significant. Add what has been said of the
ancestor of the suppliants, Epaphus, son of the Healing
Touch of Zeus : add that the Greeks, as Herodotus

tells us, traced their religion partly to Pelasgian origin
and partly to Egyptian : add that the Egyptian god,
Apis, born in the form of a heifer (conceived, as some
men said, by the lightning flash of God), was identified
by the Greeks with their own Epaphus. Read the
speech again with these things in mind, and every
word will appear full of meaning, made significant
by the whole drama, adding significance to the following scenes. If all that has been said seems fanciful,
consider the strange cry of the maidens at the height of
their supplication (when they are tearing in an ecstasy
of prayer their linen vesture) : " I implore the grace
of Hilly Apia—the outlandish utterance, well, O land,
thou kennest ! " where the outlandish utterance,
known by the land of Argos, and potent to move
her divinities, is _Āpiān Bounin_ (_gān_), "land of
Apis-Epaphus, land of Io, the cow-maiden." The
philologist may tell us that _bounis_ is "a rare word
meaning _hilly_," but to the audience, whose opinion
alone matters, it can have meant in this context
nothing but "land of the Cow."

The suppliants win the king to their side. Their
appeal as suppliants is strong. They add the proof
that they are of Argive origin, and claim protection
as the right of Io's children. Still Pelasgus hesitates.
To plunge his country into war for women is no light
matter. Then, at a highly dramatic moment, they
compel the king to yield by threatening to hang

themselves at the altar of the gods. It is a terrible threat. Suppliants dead at the altar, and those suppliants the descendants of Epaphus, whose name-sake, Apis, purified the land—such a pollution would mean divine wrath on the city and plagues far worse than any war. The king consents to plead their cause before his people, and the aid of Zeus is again invoked. The return of Danaus with the news that the hands of all the people have been raised to vote them succour, "for they heard the persuasive utter-ance of the king—but Zeus it was who brought the issue to pass" (the word used is significant, cf. 11, 12, 46, 380, 632, 697), is thus a dramatic fulfilment of prayer.

Then follows a hymn for Argos, this also made dramatic by the sequel : the ships of the pursuers are discerned approaching, and vividly described. Danaus retires : the herald, personified barbarism, comes to carry off the suppliants : when they appeal to the gods, he commits the final act of sacrilege by trying to drag the leader from the altar by her hair. All that is probably suggested more by words and music and dance than by the action : we need not stay to conjecture why fifty women are so easy a prey for one cowardly man. Anyhow, in the nick of time the king supervenes, teaches the herald to respect a Greek city, with decision but no hint of insolence undertakes to defend the maidens, but promises that Argos will allow the marriage if the suitors can persuade their cousins by fair reasons. Meanwhile he admits the suppliants to citizenship, Danaus returns with a bodyguard, of which he is exceedingly proud, and in a great procession the new citizens, now not exiled Egyptians but Greeks returned to their native land, move off, chanting praise to Zeus, praise to the gods of Argos, not without a hymn to Aphrodite. At the end of the play, as at the beginning, Zeus is invoked : and now is sounded clearly and directly the appeal which, as we have seen, gave for the audience the dramatic value of the whole performance :

> Zeus, as thou didst deliver Io, so deliver us.

THE PERSIANS

In the *Suppliants* Zeus was the champion of modesty against sacrilegious violence. When Aeschylus was in the prime of life, an event occurred which seemed to prove his righteous government of the world. The Persians rased the buildings of Athens to the ground, and threatened her state with extinction : the sequel was a new and more splendid city whose citizens were rulers of an empire. The event and the impression it made are best represented in the history of Herodotus, born just before the triumph and a favourite at Periclean Athens.

In outline his narrative is as follows. First comes a survey of the whole known world ; into it are woven stories to illustrate presumption bred by wealth, the temptation, insolence, cruelty and final ruin of the presumptuous man,—stories also (for popular morality was not clear on this point) which imply that wealth by itself involves divine jealousy and brings destruction. All peoples and tribes, including the Greeks of Asia and the islands, are seen in this world-pageant to be absorbed by the power of Persia. When Egypt is conquered, the Persian king insults the religion of the vanquished, and is smitten by madness, disaster and death. Finally Dareius, with Asia at his feet, sets his empire in order, counts his possessions as David counted his people. Now ambition led him into Europe. He invaded Scythia, was frustrated and retired, not without ominous and prophetic incident : notable for us is the bridge of boats across the Danube, preserved by the loyalty of a Greek, Histiaeus. That same man, ungratefully treated, caused the Ionians to revolt. The capital of a Persian province was burnt with Athenian aid. Now this quarrel was not the business of Athens, and for striking at the heart of Persia Athens must suffer. The vengeance was an invasion which threatened to ruin Hellas : but, at Marathon, Heracles, Athene, and the Athenian footmen wrought divine vengeance on the arrogant Dareius. At last, in the crowning act of this great epic, Xerxes, son of Dareius, yielding to ambitious dreams, spurred by evil counsellors, gathered the forces of the world and hurled them against Hellas. He rode out of Sardis between the mutilated bodies of innocent young men: he bridged the Hellespont with ships: when a storm arose and broke the bridge, he cast chains into the sea and insulted the divinity of the waters by proclaiming himself tyrant of the waves. In Greece he learnt the temper of the gods, and his host was routed at Salamis and Plataea.

The *Persians* of Aeschylus is a tragedy, not a history. The theme is Salamis, the crowning mercy, not Marathon, though that also was a triumph of Athens, nor Plataea, which was a triumph mainly of Sparta. Though Marathon is cited, as proof that Athens has already done great deeds, the Dareius of the *Persians* is not the disastrous war-lord of Marathon, but the consecrated hero-king, whose only contribution to the present calamity is that he amassed excessive wealth. The evil counsellors used this wealth as a pretext for suggestions of ambition: the wealth turned Xerxes to pride; but Dareius, so useful dramatically for the gradual revelation of disaster, is the prudent king who deplores the folly of Xerxes and gives good counsel that in future Greece be not invaded. As for Plataea, it is the result of Salamis. "The fleet's calamity hath

destroyed the host on land." Plataea and the wretched
return by Thrace and the horror of the recrossing of
the Hellespont are only the sequel and result of the
great sea-fight.

Now Salamis was the victory of the ships, the
vengeance of the sea. Poseidon once competed with
Athene for the place of patron saint to Athens, and
though Athene and her olive triumphed, he was still
venerated in the city whose glory was her ships.
Though the path of Xerxes was strewn with deeds
of insolence, the act that symbolised the spirit of
his whole invasion was the insult to the sea-god, the
chaining of the Hellespont. The note of the outraged
and avenging sea is, in fact, to this play what the
breathing of Zeus on Io is to the *Suppliants*.

The drama opens with a procession of Persian
elders, the Faithful, to give them their title, who
have been summoned by the queen mother, Atossa,
to appear before the Palace at Susa.   Their first
words are these: "We are the Faithful remnant—
Faithful as our name implies—of the Persians who
are gone to Hellas.   Warders are we of the opulent
palace rich in gold, chosen for our ripe years by none
other than king Xerxes, our lord, the son of Dareius,
to watch over his land. Our soul is stirred by presage
of ill, anxious about the return of the king and of his
army rich in gold. For all the strength, all the offspring of Asia is gone, and the king—so mutters my

heart—is young; and no messenger nor any horseman comes with news...." The words are more significant than they at first appear. The drama was produced in the eighth year after Salamis: that victory had already been celebrated by Phrynichus, and the idea of representing the mourning of Persia, not the triumph of Athens, was his. It was indeed the one device by which the theme could be treated without a display of the pride which ruined Persia. It has been suggested that some of the later speeches of the drama, where the style is less picturesque than usual, are adaptations from Phrynichus: it is certain that in the sentences just quoted Aeschylus acknowledges his debt. In the prologue of Phrynichus a eunuch, who was preparing the palace for the return of Xerxes, spoke of the "Persians who have marched against Hellas" (*bebēkotōn*). The elders start with a similar phrase, but for the colourless *marched* they substitute "*are gone,*" a word which in Greek means commonly not only "*have gone away*" but also "*are undone, have perished.*" Thus by a subtle change Aeschylus has improved his material: instead of a statement of fact, we have a poetical suggestion: the elders unconsciously sound the first note of doom. Twice in this processional the ominous word recurs: "all the strength, all the offspring of Asia is gone," and again, "such is the flower of the Persian land that is gone, her warriors for whom all Asia laments with a fierce desire, for that she reared them all; and parents and wives, with the counting of the days, shudder at the long-stretched time of their absence.' All they mean is that they are anxious about the army from which they have had no news: but their phrase means more than they know. Nor has Aeschylus done with this word: in the marching anapaests which follow the first news of defeat, this phrase, with much else in the opening scene, is recalled: the army "of much gold" has become the army "of much lamenting," and the word *oichomenōn, gone, gone,* means nothing now but "lost."

Notice further how imaginative themes are introduced and made vivid by the repetition and variation of words whose effect is cumulative. The mind is filled with suggestions of the vast horde, "terrible and countless"; of its barbarian equipment, the bow, and the chariot; of magnificence, gold, and "delicate wealth"; of the dangerous youth of the king and his unchecked authority: all themes which will be elaborated in the rest of the symphony. Finally the last words of the anapaests are most ominous of all: "Eagerly rush the dwellers by holy Tmolus" (impious in spite of their holy places) "to *cast the yoke of slavery* on Hellas." That impious eagerness is recalled in the first words of the ode which follows: "The army of the king has crossed the strait of Helle, *casting a yoke* upon the neck of the sea." And in the last stanza of the same ode this note recurs: "all the company of the footmen and the riders on horses has left this land, as a swarm of bees leaveth the hive, attendant on the captain of the host, passing over that projecting arm of the sea, the strait that belongs to both continents alike, the Hellespont now *yoked by the bridge.*"

The whole of this next ode, in fact, works these themes into new shape. Gold and the king's unchecked authority are combined in one phrase, "the god-man, ruler of the children of gold." The Persians were said to boast descent from Perseus, and Aeschylus makes that boast ominous by this allusion to the birth of the hero, conceived by Danae in a *shower of gold.* The chariot also recurs, for Xerxes is described as "urging on his Syrian car"; and the audience knew the tale of the oracle in which Apollo had foretold his ruin: "Fire shall hurl him to destruction, and the fierce war god, urging on a Syrian car."

But the central part contains the gist of the whole matter. After describing the greatness of the host, the elders cry: "No man can resist him: none is of any account who pits himself against that flood of warriors. None can check, with barriers that will stand sure, the irresistible wave of the sea: the army of the Persians is too great to be encountered, and valiant is the Persian people." The image which they have chosen to express the might of Persia is

the power of the very god against whom Xerxes has
been rash enough to declare war. Their anxiety
returns, and they add: "yet the guileful devices of
Illusion, sent by a god, what mortal shall escape?
Who is so royal that he can leap lightly out of her
toils? At first she fawns, at first she wears a face of
brightness: and so she leads the man astray into the
net of Ruin, whence mortal man cannot escape and
flee."

The so-called 'Dareius vase' (fig. 6) illustrates
the ideas which underlie this poetry. Dareius, en-
throned, is warned by one of his councillors to abandon his schemes. Below, the royal treasurer counts
the fatal wealth, coin, plate and bags of gold-dust,
and on the right Persians make the obeisance which
Greeks think unmanly and impious. Above are divine
powers involved, on the left Artemis and Apollo (with
his swan), in the centre Zeus, who points graciously
(as does a winged Victory) to Hellas, who stands
modestly with her patroness Athene: the thunderbolt is aimed at Dareius: on the right sits Asia, and
in front of her is Ἀπα(τή), *Illusion*, clad as a Fury,
holding the torches that kindle war.

The queen, who now appears, has been described
as ignorant, presumably because she asks where
Athens is. She is made to ask, of course, simply for
the sake of the reply: "Far off, towards the west,
where our lord, the sun-god wanes," an ambiguity

Fig. 6. The Tragedy of Dareius.

which in Athenian ears means "where the Persian
king, who makes himself a god, is overthrown." She
has been called a "very noble character"; but
her nobility is simply the loftiness of Aeschylean
rhetoric. In truth she is just enough a person to
be alive: character-drawing, like plot, is subordinated
to the main interest, the poem: and the poem is the
tragedy of Xerxes. She serves in fact to heighten
our sense of the splendour and temptation in which
he lived. Like all her people, she puts Xerxes first,
the army only second: that is because she is a Persian,
and a Persian queen. Her maternal feeling adds
pathos, and gives the play much of its tone of
chivalry, the *aidôs* [αἰδώς] of the triumphant Greek.
She has been described also as superstitious, and this
is an important point. Her reverence for Xerxes is
certainly superstitious, and, like the elders, she is
intended to behave in oriental fashion; but her belief
in dreams and omens and ghost-raising is not superstition for Aeschylus: we also must believe if we are
to appreciate. Her dream is a genuine and divine
revelation of disaster. In form it is a treatment
of the yoke and chariot motives, and a summing up
in verbal tableau of the rest of the play. She has
seen Xerxes in a vision "bending two fair women
beneath the yoke of his chariot." These women
stand for the Greeks of Asia and the Athenians. The
latter "break the yoke in twain," "my son falls and his

father, Dareius, rises at his side, pitying him: and
when he sees him, Xerxes rends his garments." The
portent again which she saw when she was "purging
the dream" was an eagle torn by a hawk, flying to
the altar of Apollo. That is to say, she saw the
royal bird, the emblem of Persian kings, flying to
the altar of Apollo, whose shrine at Delphi Xerxes
had tried to plunder, and mangled, the great bird by
the small, by the hawk that was sacred to Apollo.
To believe in such a portent was common sense.
And she unconsciously drives home its significance
by her final euphemism: "Be his fortune good, men
must marvel at his greatness: be it bad, he is still
under no authority; no city is his master; for if he
himself survive, he is, as ever, master of his land."
Precisely: that position is what led to his undoing.
The only possible advice is that of the elders: to pray
to gods above and powers below, especially to Dareius,
a powerful friend in the grave.

A survivor of the sea-fight brings the first news of
defeat. It is a trace of primitive construction that he
addresses the chorus, not the queen. But the silence
of Atossa makes her speech effective when it comes.
In the sailor's short sentences to which the elders
reply in bursts of song, we hear again old motives,
wealth, numbers and the sea. A passage of some
difficulty may be quoted: "The coasts of Salamis
with every place that is neighbour to them are

crammed with unhappy (unburied) dead." "Alas:
the bodies of our beloved, carried, so your words
imply, up and down in the wandering tides, dipped
and dipped again" (a grim metaphor from the rich
dyed robes of orientals), "sea-buffeted." The words
"in the wandering tides" *planktois en diplakessi*
[πλαγκτοῖς ἐν διπλάκεσσι] are vague and not trans-
lateable: the vagueness, I think, is deliberate, and the
audience are meant to think of the straits of Salamis
and also of the Hellespont and the bridge. The
sailor adds his comment: "Aye, the bow availed
nothing: and all the host was perishing, victims of
the charging of ship on ship." The narrative follows;
disaster piled on disaster, Xerxes the victim of divine
illusion, the Greeks guided by the gods, the Persians,
like slaves, driven into battle under threat of be-
heading, but the Greeks advancing with that song
that saved at Salamis, "O sons of Greece, go, set
your Country free."

After the lament which ensues, Atossa, who has
retired, appears in garb of mourning. A solemn
incantation follows. By prayers to powers of the
underworld the spirit of Dareius is set free: by
lamentation his sympathy is roused: by flattery he
is propitiated: finally by a touch of reproach at
the end he is reminded of Marathon and goaded
into activity. So at length the hero king appears.
Like the sailor, he first addresses the chorus:

but the reverence of the elders forbids them to answer, and he turns to his queen as the only person who dares hold converse with him: thus Aeschylus has again turned old convention to dramatic use.

It has been remarked that the king displays a "strange condition of mind": that he "blames Xerxes chiefly for chaining the Hellespont" and for destroying the shrines of the gods: and that when asked for advice, he only suggests that there shall be no more invasions of Greece. I need hardly say that in the poem these things are not defects. The "strangest thing he does," says Mr Sidgwick, "is to interrupt the pressing question of what the Persians are to do now with a brief enumeration of the Persian and Median kings." The criticism would be just if this were a modern play: but really there is no pressing question for the Persians: the purpose of the historical lecture is the purpose of the whole scene;—to vivify the situation, to point the moral. The ancient kings were godly and prospered: Cyaxares "completed his work, for wisdom was at the helm of his heart": "the gods hated not Cyrus, since he was wise and moderate"; Cambyses "guided the people" (we hear nothing, of course, about his sin and ruin), but Mardes, "a disgrace to his fatherland and the ancient throne, was slain by guile." "I myself, though I made many expeditions, brought no such evil as this upon the city." Such a speech is not in any important sense undramatic.

Having revealed the evils yet in store, "the fount of woe still gushing forth," the ghost departs; not without further suggestion of orientalism in the command to Atossa to prepare robes for Xerxes, who has torn his royal vesture in his grief. She too departs, and in her final words sums up her rôle: "How many bitter griefs are coming upon me! Most of all doth this thing wound me,—the shame of the misused robes about the body of my son." She does not appear again, for attention must be concentrated on Xerxes. Before his entry the praise of Dareius is sung in an ode which makes us forget Marathon, and think of him only as "the aged monarch, author of no ill," the king who sought not war. This also throws into relief the figure of Xerxes, for whom the elders have no such words. They have no comfort for him, as he stands disgraced before them, nothing but lamentation and questions which are really upbraidings. The justification of this final scene is our sense of the greatness of Persian kings, created by the whole drama, not least by the apparition of Dareius: the measure of greatness is the measure of the fall. The gorgeous robes of Persia, her riches and her bowmen, have been used throughout as poetical themes: now, when the elders cry: "What of the Persian host has escaped destruction?"

the king replies: "Look on the remnant here—all
that remains of my vesture—and this quiver—the
treasury of my weapons—empty."

The Seven against Thebes

Five years after the production of *The Persians,*
appeared the trilogy of the House of Laius, whose
third part is known to us as *The Seven against Thebes.*
At that time, when Athens was refortifying the Acro-
polis, this story of a famous siege must have had a
strong appeal. But the play is most interesting as
an example of an important Aeschylean motive, the
family curse which descends from father to son. The
first two parts are lost, but we can gather their general
import from a chorus of the *Seven* (l. 728).

Apollo by an oracle forbade Laius, the king, to
beget a child: he disobeyed, begat Oedipus, and
exposed the child to die on the mountains in the
hope that so he might avoid the consequences of his
sin. But with the begetting of Oedipus the Curse
was begotten: the son survived, and, returning without knowledge of his parentage, slew his father, saved
the city by answering the riddle of the Sphinx, married
his mother, begat children by her and became king
of his father's city. When he learnt what he had
done, he blinded himself, and in rage at some

conduct of his children cursed them with the prayer "that they should divide their inheritance with the sword." The sons, to avoid the curse, agreed to hold kingship in alternate years, and the younger, Polyneices, went abroad for the first year. When the year expired, Eteocles refused to give up the throne, and Polyneices brought against his own city an army led by seven chieftains from the Peloponnese. The curse of Oedipus is fulfilled in our play by the meeting and mutual slaughter of the brothers.

In the trilogy there were three stages, and in each the curse was seen at work with wider consequences. First, Laius sinned and was himself cut off: Oedipus was the instrument of destruction as the begetting of him was the act of sin. In the second part, the downfall of Oedipus involved the family, the mother-wife, and the two sons whom he cursed in sudden wrath, just as in sudden wrath ("madly," say the chorus) he had slain his father. Finally, in our play, the whole city is in peril of destruction: she is saved, but Eteocles and Polyneices are lost. Our concern is with the city as well as with the hero. According to his usual method Aeschylus takes and elaborates a familiar image. The city is a ship in peril, Eteocles the captain on whose prudence safety depends.

The first words, as usual, provide a key to the drama. "Citizens of Cadmus' city," says the king, "the man who guides the tiller of the state, whose

care directs her action, must, if he be a trusty helms-
man, speak (as well as act) with seemliness." In the
previous play the audience had heard Oedipus curse
his sons; an outburst of unruly words had involved
the family in ruin. The whole trilogy depends on the
ancient feeling that the spoken word has power to
affect events for good and evil. Disobedience to an
oracle destroyed Laius: angry words destroyed the
house of Oedipus: now our attention is directed to
the words of Eteocles. It is on words, not on military
dispositions, that the fate of the city hangs: the besiegers are defeated because of their presumptuous
language and boastful ensigns: the city is saved
because her warriors, as represented by the king, are
free from arrogance and vaunting. Yet Eteocles, we
know, is doomed, and the victim of an hereditary
taint is not, in Aeschylus, ruined without offences of
his own. Eteocles, by his virtue saves the city, and
his tragedy is great because by modesty he himself
so nearly escapes. Throughout there are hints of a
passionate nature, held in check, but held in check
with difficulty. In the final test (his brother's impious challenge to the duel), anger and false honour
break the barriers of self-restraint; his virtue snaps,
and he rushes wilfully to his doom.

The drama falls into three divisions, in each of
which a situation is created by a messenger. The
first announces that the besiegers have decided on a

general attack : seven chieftains are to assault the
seven gates, and the army is already moving. At this
point there rushes into the dancing-floor no stately
procession such as we witnessed in the *Suppliants*
and *Persians,* but a rout of women stricken with
a panic-terror, divine, but of ill omen for the city.
Their screams and wild appeals are the first test of
Eteocles : his impulse is to anger, and his first upbraidings savour of impiety : but he controls himself,
and finally, by exhorting them to pray in Hellenic
fashion (in orderly array and with well-omened words),
he soothes them and recovers moral strength. Thus
the first part of our play at once makes vivid the
peril and the terror of the city, and reveals the
character of Eteocles, a noble nature but over-
passionate.

The second messenger describes the champions
with a rhetoric which is, as Euripides pointed out in
the *Phoenissae,* quite ludicrous from the military point
of view, and indefensible as drama if the military
arrangements really matter. Nor is it enough to
say that Athenians loved descriptive oratory and
were interested in the heroes and in heraldry. The
point is that the boasts and blazons of the champions
convict them of presumption, and doom them before-
hand to failure. The answers of Eteocles are always
right, take advantage of the enemy's insolence, and
secure divine favour by studied moderation : and in

each case, after the speech of the messenger and the reply of the king, the chorus clench the situation with a short lyrical prayer. Each of these triads of two speeches and a lyric is dramatic: for in each Eteocles is tested and not found wanting: yet we know that in the final test he will not stand. The sixth champion is Amphiaraus, the wise seer, who foresees disaster and is opposed to the impious attack: of him Eteocles speaks no word of evil, and his noble treatment of this noble enemy makes a contrast with the crisis which immediately follows. The seventh champion is the king's own brother, crying that against Eteocles he is come, and Eteocles he means to slay. Then the restraint of Eteocles gives way: he answers taunt with taunt, calls for his armour, declares that there is no other way but to go himself against his brother. When the chorus urge that it is sin, that it will be a pollution not to be expiated, his answer is that honour drives him. The chorus see that he is possessed by the madness of sinful rage: he knows that he is going to death: but with an impious fatalism he goes, crying out that the curse of his father is fulfilled.

On this view there is surely no lack of drama in the central scene: and the view is confirmed by the chorus, who at this juncture stress the significance of the event by tracing the work of the curse from Laius to Oedipus, from Oedipus to his sons. A third messenger appears with a double tale: the city is saved (he repeats the phrase), at six gates all is well: "the seventh is captured," but not by the enemy,—"by the King Apollo himself, who thus fulfils upon the children of Oedipus the ancient sin of Laius." The brothers have fallen, each by the other's hand.

The lamentations follow. Two trains of mourning women attend the brothers: Ismene and Antigone lead the wailing, the former attendant on Eteocles, the latter on Polyneices. That completes the drama. But tradition demands something more. A herald announces that the traitor Polyneices, besieger of his own city, is condemned to hatred even after death: no one is to give him burial. Antigone and her train declare that they will disobey: and so the traditional story of the heroism of Antigone is used as a device for the symmetrical arrangement of the procession. The mourners fall into two columns, and move off chanting the solemn anapaests which we missed in the first wild entry of the chorus.

PROMETHEUS

The lofty conception of Zeus which we found in the *Suppliants* is of course inconsistent with the legend of a god with human passions who forces the unhappy Io to his will. Religion finds satisfaction in the thought that after suffering Io was blessed ; but other legends, also current as divinely inspired utterances of poets, were even more difficult to reconcile with the conception of a moral god. Zeus had won his empire by force: he had deposed and thrown into chains his father Cronos: Cronos himself had deposed and mutilated his father Ouranos. To establish the reign of Zeus a whole generation of older gods had been oppressed. Prometheus, the personification of wisdom, one of the elder race, had aided Zeus to his throne, yet he offended the new god and was barbarously tortured. Thus the legends, shifting and inconsistent, the product of conflict and compromise between different tribes and customs, are clear in their portrayal of Zeus as a tyrant who has won and kept his power by violence and lawlessness. Yet this rebel against gods, parents, lawful right, was for Aeschylus, and in some degree for all Athenians, the sanction and upholder of Greek morality,—"Honour the gods, your parents and the laws." The legends were imaginations of an age which demanded no morality in its gods. When Zeus was conceived as moral, the religious poet must still present the legendary Zeus: otherwise his god would be an abstraction of philosophy, no possible object for popular religion. Yet the legends appeared directly to contradict the doctrine of divine perfection.

In such a case a modern theologian might treat the legend as half untrue : he might speak of a progressive revelation, saying that men have discarded unworthy conceptions of God, who has always been, as He is now, just and merciful and pure. That is not the method of Aeschylus. Instead of a progressive revelation he conceived, with noble audacity, of a progressive God. Zeus himself illustrates the law "that the path of learning is through suffering." He was once at war with right, at war with fate ; he is now identified with righteousness, subject no doubt to fate, yet identified with fate, since what he wills is now the "effortless harmony." The history of religion seems to show that Aeschylus has lighted upon a profound poetical truth. The truth is indeed poetical, and it is idle to attempt to square the Aeschylean Zeus with logic : as in the case of Io, so here, the justification of Zeus is in poetry and emotion, not to be expressed in syllogistic argument.

The legend of Prometheus in the form which Aeschylus selected is the strongest conceivable indictment of the traditional Zeus. Aeschylus does not, like Pindar, slur over grosser details of his myth. Indeed the case against Zeus is so finely presented that, in the absence of the subsequent drama, scholars have thought a justification impossible. They underestimate the power of poetry and of piety alike. We have here to consider what has survived, the indictment of Zeus: but we are not to suppose that the trilogy as a whole contradicted the religion which underlies all the poetry of Aeschylus.

Prometheus was worshipped as the giver of fire, and with fire of all the arts which make a good life possible. According to the legend chosen by Aeschylus that fire was stolen from Zeus: it was given to men in spite of Zeus, who wished to destroy the human race. Prometheus pitied man and defied the tyrant who would destroy him. For that crime alone he was punished. The motive is like that of the story of the Fall in Genesis: the serpent, who was "more subtil than any beast of the field," was cursed by God because he had made men taste of Knowledge, "a tree to be desired to make one wise":—so that, as the Lord God said, "Behold the man is become as one of us." There are further parallels, but the point which we must here notice is this, that it is possible for religion to outgrow its mythical dress. Until intelligence is clear and the morality of the stories is called in question, men can believe at once in a good God and in legends which imply that God is jealous of the wisdom of man.

Zeus then is represented as himself learning wisdom through experience: the legendary fact which is used as symbol of this process is a secret known only to Prometheus, a danger of which Prometheus alone can warn the god: the secret is that

Zeus, unless he is warned by Prometheus, will unite
with a certain woman and produce a child more
powerful than himself.   In terms of religion this
means that Zeus at first relied too much on strength,
and that, to be reconciled with fate, he needed
moderation and wisdom.   On the other hand Prometheus also had to learn: his theft of fire was noble,
and it is difficult to realise how he erred ; but it is
probable that our play is the second of the trilogy,
and that in the first part he was represented as in
need of discipline.   The daughters of Ocean think
him over-stubborn, and Greek morality insisted on
the duty of submission to the inevitable as such.
More important is the fact that in Greek thought sin
and error tend to be identified.   Prometheus himself (l. 282) admits that he has erred : " By my own
will I erred, I deny it not : in aiding mortals I brought
trouble on myself.   Yet I thought not that the penalty
would be such as this ": in other words Prometheus
acted without that full measure of forethought which
was necessary for his perfect justification.   Prometheus was Wisdom, but his wisdom was made
more perfect by suffering.

The scene is placed with geographical vagueness,
but poetical exactness, in the Scythian mountains
towards the Caucasus, on the bounds of Europe and
Asia.   Here "at the farthest bounds of earth, in a
lonely waste where no foot has trodden," the son of

righteous Earth is bound and tortured by the Father of Heaven. The background to the tragedy of Zeus is the whole universe: the characters are gods and men and powers of nature. In no Greek play is atmosphere so vividly suggested: in none is the imagination so filled with the beauty and terror of nature and of life.

An ancient argument gives the following summary: "From Prometheus, bound in Scythia because of the theft of fire, Io, on her wanderings, learns that when she arrives in Egypt she will bear Epaphus from the laying on of hands of Zeus: Hermes is introduced threatening Prometheus that he will be struck by the thunderbolt if he does not reveal what is destined to happen to Zeus: finally there is a thunderstorm and Prometheus disappears." The summary is meagre, but it suggests the fact, not always appreciated, that Io is essential to the play. A brief analysis will show that her entrance marks a crisis in the drama, and that its moment is carefully chosen.

Though Prometheus, the central, all-absorbing figure, is inflexible towards Zeus, the drama depends on changes of his mood. He is silent to the taunts of Kratos (Strength), and the pity of his torturer Hephaestus. Left utterly alone, he breaks silence in his astonishing appeal to earth and sky and sea. The Nymphs of Ocean heard the rivetting of his chains, but poetically their coming is a response to his cry.

Their sympathy moves him to tell the story of his
fatal love for men : his mood is melting. But Oceanus,
the trimmer, who shakes a sage head of disapproval
and offers to intercede with Zeus, is sternly dismissed :
even here, however, stress is laid on the motive of
unselfishness : Prometheus will not allow Oceanus
to embroil himself on his behalf. The songs of the
Nymphs are first of the travail of all nature in
sympathy for Prometheus, then of the weakness of
men and of the sorrow for Prometheus of all mankind. Thus, as in the *Suppliants*, we were led from
invocation of divine aid to the securing of human
allies, so, in this greater drama, we are shown first
the spectacle of the suffering silent god, alone on a
mountain-side, deserted by god and man : he cries to
nature, and she responds, first in the coming of the
Nymphs, then in the universal mourning of Nature
which their song suggests : the song changes and we
are made to feel that mankind is also suffering with
the hero, yet unable to aid him or abate his pain.
At this supreme moment, when the mortal inhabitants
of earth have been brought into the imaginative background, Io appears, one of the human victims of Zeus.
The tales of Io's past and future wanderings are introduced not merely because to Athenians of this age, as
to the Elizabethans, the whole world had a glamour
of romance, but also because through them the whole
world is poetically brought into relation with the

suffering god. This geographical rhetoric is as relevant to the poetical drama as is the world-pageant of Herodotus to his epic of the Persian war. Finally pity for Io wrings from Prometheus the prophecy of Epaphus and Heracles. As the release of Io is to come through the bearing of Epaphus, so from that birth shall spring the hero who is to deliver Prometheus.

The hints of the mysterious fate that threatens Zeus have grown more and more significant. At length they have been heard in heaven, and Hermes, the messenger of Zeus, descends to extort the secret by threats or by persuasion. The wrath of Prometheus now inspires his noblest defiance. At this moment of extreme torture, as he is hurled into Tartarus, wracked with pain and with the prospect of pain, his triumph is greatest. The refusal of the Nymphs to leave him, though they are engulfed with him in ruin, is a recurrence of the romantic note which has made the drama a poem of exquisite beauty, not an unlovely morality. Without this touch the tragedy would be harsher but also less sublime. How great is the imagination and the skill of composition is shown by this:—that although the Nymphs add loveliness and tenderness to the catastrophe, their fate does not distract attention from Prometheus. Our emotion at the end, as always, is for the hero: but the emotion is subtly modified, the hero is made more wonderful by the love which he inspires.

THE STORY OF ORESTES

Orestes, son and avenger of Agamemnon, was to the Greeks a righteous slayer, a destroyer of iniquity, like Heracles or Perseus. The story in the earliest form which can be traced is this : Atreus, son of Pelops, a king, rich, but of a stock already under a curse (see fig. 7), hated and banished his brother Thyestes, who had plotted against him and seduced his wife : pretending to be reconciled, he recalled his brother and entertained him at a feast, causing him to eat the bodies of his own sons : Thyestes ate, learned the nature of the food, cursed Atreus and his house, and went back into exile. One son, Aegisthus, survived to avenge him : when Agamemnon, son of Atreus, had succeeded to his father's throne and was absent on an expedition against Troy, Aegisthus seduced his wife and usurped his power : Agamemnon on his return was murdered by Aegisthus and the unfaithful wife. At length Orestes slew Aegisthus and the woman, and so won back his father's possessions.

This crude tale of murder and revenge dates from an age before the city had superseded the clan. A murder polluted the victim's clan : his clansmen were bound to slay the murderer. Souls of men violently slain were supposed to wander wretchedly, perhaps to inhabit again the corpse,

Fig. 7. The engendering of the Curse in the House of Pelops. Pelops defeated Œnomaus and won Hippodameia as his bride by the aid of Myrsilus, the charioteer of Œnomaus. Instead of rewarding Myrsilus he flung him into the sea (here symbolised by the dolphin), and Myrsilus cursed him. The Curse is seen as a winged fury, hovering over Pelops, with a drawn sword in her right hand and the scabbard in her left.

certainly to bring plagues upon the kinsmen until the death was avenged. The slayer was pursued not only by the human avenger, but by the dead man's self, or the dark Ministers of Earth, the Furies, stirred up by the curse of the murdered man. Each slaying, therefore, led to a retributive murder: a life demanded a life. A curse, moreover, was inherited like property: it belonged to the whole clan, and might ruin a victim who had committed no trespass of his own. So the old legend is like the tale of a Corsican—or Kentucky—vendetta, made more terrible by superstitious belief in the power of the dead man and the fatal effect of a curse.

Hesiod and inspired sages before him preached the justice of the gods. The Olympian religion, particularly that of Apollo at Delphi, brought aid to mortal distress. Ritual of purification, sacrifice for blood, were substituted for the ancient feud: oracles revealed the will of the gods, showed something of the future, made clear at least the path by which a man, whatever his fate, might walk wisely as befits a mortal. Under Delphic influences, it appears, the story of Orestes was retold: the oracle enjoined upon him the killing which was the just punishment of crime: the god purified him and gave him absolution: but Orestes had shed blood, and the god must defend his servant not only from the human avenger but also from the wrathful nether powers: Apollo with his arrows routed the Erinyes. That is the explanation of the first scene of the *Eumenides* where Apollo, having purified Orestes, drives the Furies with threats and reviling from his temple (cf. fig. 8).

Fig. 8. Apollo (accompanied by his sister, the huntress Artemis) purifies Orestes with the blood of a pig. On the left a Fury rises from the earth, and two other Furies are aroused from sleep by the ghost of Clytaemnestra. Orestes holds the sword with which he slew his mother.

But conscience is not satisfied by ritual purification. A citizen of Athens is a free and a responsible moral being : he is judged by reasonable

laws, by judges who are citizens and free. According
to Attic legend Orestes was not freed until he had
been tried before the ancient court of Areopagus:
the votes were equal for acquittal and for condemna-
tion: Athene herself gave a casting vote for acquittal, and thus established the Athenian rule of
law, that acquittal followed an equality of votes.
Aeschylus gives greater significance to this incident:
according to him Athene founded the Areopagus for
this trial. Her gift to Athens was the institution of
free human justice: that is why she is greater than
Apollo, and greater than the Furies.

In the version of Aeschylus the moral issue is
completely altered and the figure of Orestes made
intensely tragic by the stress laid on the mother-
murder. Aegisthus was in early tradition the murderer: the vengeance was on him: Clytaemnestra
was his instrument or accomplice and duly suffered
with him. Now she has become the criminal, doing
her will for her own ends upon her husband. The
feast of Thyestes, the hate and meanness of Aegisthus,
the ancient curse in the house, are used to heighten
the effect: but the deed is the deed of Clytaemnestra, and the thing that is enjoined upon Orestes
is the killing not of Aegisthus, the old enemy of the
blood-feud, but of the murderous wife, his mother
Clytaemnestra. The *Agamemnon* is the presentation
of her crime.

All the plays which have been discussed contribute to the understanding of this great work. As in the *Suppliants*, the choral odes are essential to the drama, though here the dialogue has reached dramatic perfection. As in the *Suppliants*, the *Persians*, the *Prometheus*, the theme involves the double imagination of Greece and of a distant foreign land : when the *Agamemnon* opens, the king is far away besieging oriental Troy : the beacons flash news of his triumph across the intervening sea : he arrives and shows that he, a Greek, can behave like the oriental kings of Troy : and as their doom was, such is his. As in the *Persians*, wealth and the pride which it engenders are a recurrent theme and menace. As in the *Seven*, the note of an inherited curse is heard, though here, even more clearly than in the earlier play, it is the sin of the individual, not the inherited taint, which causes final ruin. The *Prometheus* will help us to understand the hints, significant in the *Agamemnon*, but only developed fully in the *Eumenides*, of ancient Titanic powers, justly deposed yet not justly to be dishonoured by the younger gods, needing to be reconciled with their successors before a moral universe or a justly human piety is possible. Finally, throughout the trilogy, as in all the plays, there are recurrent themes, images, symbols, moral ideas, which are woven into the web of the poem and contribute

more than any mechanism of plot to the unity and
power of the design.

With triumphant art the death of Agamemnon
is made an important event, tragic and divinely
ordered : it, like all the rest, is part of the will of
Zeus, mysterious but just. Yet Clytaemnestra is the
dominant figure : our sense of the moral significance of Agamemnon's fall does not diminish but
rather heightens our feeling of the wilful guilt of
Clytaemnestra. Agamemnon sinned when he sacri-
ficed his daughter Iphigeneia : a goddess demanded
it, a prophet enjoined it, yet it was a crime: here in
the background is an inconsistency which the poet,
being a poet, need not trouble to explain : the effect
of this unholy sacrifice was to increase the danger of
the king who was already threatened by the curse
of his rich but ill-starred race. Such deeds breed
a mood of reckless, passionate pride. He captured
Troy and at the moment of triumph temptation
came. Distraction (Ate) lured her victim into the
net of destruction by enticing him to an act of insolence.   He returned home with Cassandra, the
priestess of Apollo, as his concubine : that in itself
was impious : but the final symbol of his pride,
dramatically sufficient by itself to cause the ruin of
so prosperous a king, was the tacit likening of himself to a god when at the persuasion of Clytaemnestra (who is at this point the instrument of Ate,

the personification of fawning Peitho) he passed
triumphant into his palace walking on purple, meet
only for the service of the gods.

The significance of all this is heightened by the

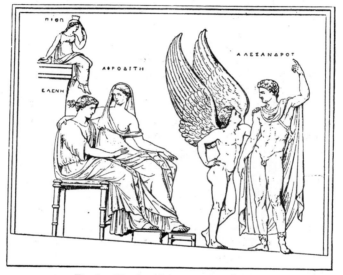

Fig. 9.   The fatal love of Paris and Helen.

memory of the Persian wars: that struggle was regarded as the sequel and counterpart of the ancient
conflict between East and West.   When the gods
had overthrown the insolence of Persia some of the

She hated him for his unfaithfulness: yet she too
was unfaithful. Cassandra we have seen and pitied:
Clytaemnestra's paramour is Aegisthus, mean and
cowardly. The king is weak and well-meaning: his
death moves us greatly because of the greatness of
his situation, and of achievements which we hear
but do not witness. Clytaemnestra is strong and
wilful: she is great because her crime is great, her
character greatly evil. She is indeed Temptation,
the tool of designing Ate: she is indeed the embodi-
ment of the Curse that haunts the house: she is also
a woman, cruel, calculating, ironic, masterful, resolute
—supremely therefore guilty.

What has been said of Paris throughout the play
points not only to Agamemnon but to her: when
with unbroken courage, but with a sick heart, she
has quelled the angry citizens, and has led her
paramour by the door through which she enticed her
husband, into the palace where she is now supreme,

> For something cloaked within the night the mind
> Stands listening:—the divine eyes are not blind
> To men of blood: the man of mere success,
> Luck's thriver in defect of Righteousness,
> Doomed by the dark Avengers, wanes again at last,
> Dwindling, until he fades out where the dim
> Lost shadows are; and there, no help for him.

In the *Choephoroe* or *Libation-Pourers to the
Dead* Orestes the avenger slays his mother. The

incomparable greatness of *Agamemnon* as a human drama is likely to make a modern reader feel that in the sequel interest flags. Orestes, for example, owes his tragic interest mainly to his situation : he is not, like Clytaemnestra, a vividly imagined person. The reason is that Aeschylus intentionally keeps him impersonal in order that Apollo and no other may be felt to be the author of the terrible deed. The balance was, so to speak, corrected for the audience by the fact that Orestes, not his mother, was the central figure in the legend. Indeed, much else besides the figure of Orestes must have lost for us significance with the loss of earlier poetry on which the drama is founded and to which it constantly alludes. The dream of Clytaemnestra, the meeting of Orestes and Electra at the tomb, the faithful servant, the figure of Pylades, friend of the hero and representative of Apollo (who speaks only once, and that at the supreme moment, to remind Orestes of the divine command): all these are apparently familiar to the audience, and doubly effective from the associations which they recall. Moreover, the effect of this play depend on beliefs and ritual now strange or forgotten in Western Europe. We must believe that the murdered king is potent in the grave: that the plagues which Apollo foretold as the consequence of disobedience were not more but less appalling than would actually have been inflicted:

that incantation really stirs the dead, and rouses the
avenging spirit to give strength to his son : that
Orestes at the end of the drama really sees the Furies.
But that also is not enough: throughout the play
there are allusions, which will escape us unless we
look for them, to the most sacred rites of Attic
religion, the holy mysteries of Eleusis, wherein were
displayed the symbols of life after death, of light after
darkness.   "For something cloaked within the night
the mind stood listening," and Orestes comes "as a
light kindled in the house."   The morning breaks and
the shadows flee away.

But Orestes must suffer.   Even as he stands in
triumph where Clytaemnestra stood, with the bodies
of his mother and her paramour before him where
once lay Agamemnon and Cassandra ; even as he
spreads 'out for his justification the witness of his
mother's guilt, the purple robe in which she wrapped
her victim, which is also, poetically, the broidery on
which he walked to his destruction, the net of Ate,
the hunting-snare for Agamemnon, the winding-sheet
of Clytaemnestra ;—his voice falters, his words go
astray: he cries to Apollo, yet madness takes him :
he himself is in the toils, and the Erinyes of his
mother's wrath drive him from the home which he
has freed.

The moral problem of Orestes is really inso-
luble.   As the son of the murdered man he was

bound to slay the murderer: that was clear to
Athenians: for in Attic law, though the state adjudged the guilt and superintended the punishment,
the old doctrine still prevailed that a murdered
man demanded satisfaction, and the kinsmen must
avenge. None but the next of kin might prosecute:
the assurance that he would act was the wrath of the
dead and the pollution which would come if the
blood were not avenged. On the other hand, in
slaying his father's murderers Orestes had slain his
mother: that, in spite of clan and fatherhood and
Apollo, in spite even of Athene, could not be tolerated
if it were the last word of the play. Orestes disappears from sight and almost from mind before the
end of the *Eumenides*. Even Athene's vote and her
argument that father-right is higher than the right
of motherhood, would be frigid if it stood alone,
though we must remember that to piety such an
argument is not futile. Athene is the goddess of the
city, sprung by a miraculous generation from the
head of the highest god: whether or not reminiscences of the victory of patriarchy over matriarchy
add to its significance, an appeal to that divine event,
the birth of a goddess begotten not conceived, must
not be dismissed as trivial. Yet the Furies are still
unreconciled: all the poet's art is needed if we are to
feel that Zeus has wrought all to a righteous end.
So the conclusion of the matter is not the justification

of Orestes, but the glorifying of Athenian law and
Athenian religion.

In the first place Aeschylus has made the trial of
Orestes the occasion of the founding of the Areopagus. Secondly, by the spell of Persuasion (a new
and profound use of the word which has recurred so
often with so sinister a meaning) Athene wins the Furies
to friendship for her city: they become *Eumenides*,
the *kindly goddesses*, and are escorted in procession
to the home in which they are to be honoured, their
cave-shrine on the slope of Areopagus. Already
every man in the theatre knew of the *dread goddesses*,
mysterious powers of earth, " Givers of Good and
Evil," annually propitiated by a solemn procession.
Already they were regarded as witnesses of trials
judged on the Hill of Ares, as sanctioners of just
retribution and punishers of false oaths. But probably Aeschylus was the first to identify these
goddesses with the Furies, the Avengers of kindred
blood. He was greatly daring to present in bodily
shape those awful forms : for the terror which, according to the well-known story, their appearance
inspired, was due less to their frightful aspect than
to the belief that such beings had real existence and
were potent to harm. The poet was justified when,
by the reconciliation with Athene, he showed how the
goddess shields her citizens from dangerous powers.
In the wise Athenian city the terrors of nameless

mysteries are transformed. All the justice of the Erinyes, all the light and cleansing of Apollo, are absorbed, not superseded by the free, just, human Areopagus, sanctioned by powers of heaven and of the under-world alike.

Yet that is not all. In 458 B.C., when the trilogy was produced, the Areopagus had just emerged from a great political struggle. After the Persian wars the aristocratic party had dominated the state by means of the Areopagus, which still possessed political as well as judicial powers. After fierce conflict, the leaders of the new democracy, Ephialtes and his greater ally, Pericles, had stripped the ancient Council of its other power, but had left to it the sacred right of judging murder. In the struggle Ephialtes had been murdered : Cimon, the leader of the aristocrats had been exiled. But all that was past. In glorifying the Areopagus in respect of the powers which it still retained, Aeschylus celebrates a reconciliation of all Athens. In the final procession the Eumenides are invested in scarlet robes such as were worn by resident aliens at Athens in the greatest public festival of the state : by the language and ritual Aeschylus recalls the Panathenaic procession, whose glory was to be carved by Pheidias on the Parthenon at the will of Pericles. Add that Orestes, at his acquittal, promised to Athene's city the eternal friendship of his own : and that Athens had lately

entered into fresh alliance with Argos.   With the
thought of all these things, and the sight of Athene
herself, glorified even above the god of Delphi,
maintaining justice yet driving out vain terror,
approving the alliances and laws of her citizens,
and finally directing her own procession, the symbol
of the reconciliation of the tragedy and also of the
union and good destiny of Athens,—we may believe
that the conclusion of the trilogy, whatever its logic,
was poetically not unjustified.

CHAPTER IV

SOPHOCLES

It is a commonplace that moderation is the central notion of Greek moralising, and proportion the characteristic merit of Greek building and statuary. Plato followed the instinct of an Athenian gentleman when he thought of justice as a harmony among the elements of the soul. Happiness lies, according to Greek proverbs, in avoidance of excess. A good man has a fair mind in a beautiful body, and is content with moderate prosperity, reasonable freedom, sound sense but not too great curiosity or knowledge. For the city the ideal is also a just proportion : she should be free but not lawless, pious but not superstitious, valiant yet not, like Sparta, a camp of perpetual hardship, cultivated yet not, like Asiatic cities, effeminate. That is the ideal to which Thucydides looked back when he made Pericles claim for Athens that she was a teacher and a pattern to all Hellas. "We love beauty, yet we are simple : we love wisdom, but our manliness is not impaired....By our own intelligence we see or judge what is right to be done. Reason is not, we think, a hindrance to action ; the true hindrance is to omit the discipline of thought before proceeding to the necessary act." For some thirty years of her prosperity, when the Olympian Pericles guided her democracy and beautified the city, Athens appeared to her noblest citizens to have attained that perfect balance which is the best that mortals can achieve. Among the "Lovers of Athens" who have recorded that sense of great achievement the greatest are Pheidias whose Parthenon was finished seven years before the outbreak of the fatal war, Thucydides whose history of that war is dominated by the memory of Periclean Athens, and the poet Sophocles.

The picture of Sophocles which is handed down by the ancients is perhaps idealised, and modern commentators by suppressing certain anecdotes have refined still further the gold of his reputation. To Athenians he seemed typical of the happy period in which his prime was lived. As a youth he is said to have been chosen for his beauty as the leader of the choir which celebrated Salamis. Naked and anointed, bearing an ivory lyre, he is said to have led the dance. However that may be, it is agreed that he was beautiful, and an exquisite musician : for as a young man he won honour by his ball-playing when he appeared in one of his own dramas as Nausicaa ; and as Thamyris, who vied with Apollo in music, he won glory by his harping. He was amiable, witty, a charming companion, a generous rival. By no means austere, nor averse to light and fashionable loves, he became in his ripe old age a model of all that an old man should be : there is no excuse for the suggestion that his loves are imaginations of the comic poets : had he been more austere he would have been (at least to Athenian minds) less amiable. He may or he may not have had trouble of a domestic kind, the result of jealousy between his son by a lawful wife and his son by a concubine. In other respects his life was fortunate. When his first tragedy was produced he was only twenty-seven years old : Plutarch relates the pleasant legend that the victorious Cimon and his colleagues were invited to adjudge the prize, and awarded it to Sophocles. He continued to produce throughout his long life, and was always first or second of the three competitors. He did not allow poetry to make him a bad citizen, but held high office in peace and war, without disgrace if not with great distinction. His means were abundant, and it is hinted that he was not too lavish in spending : his family was gifted in poetry like himself : he was the friend of Herodotus, of Pericles, of Ion the Chian poet : it is not recorded that he was intimate with Anaxagoras, but he seems to have been acquainted with the opinions of philosophers without being addicted to a dangerous pursuit of speculative truth. He died in Athens without lingering sickness: both Aeschylus and Euripides had died in voluntary exile. His death came happily before the ruin of Athens. He had been pious in life, and had brought to Athens the cult of Asclepius the Healer: after death he was worshipped as the hero-host of Asclepius. And it was said that he had been happy in life and death.

His generation, his temperament and his life correspond remarkably to the general nature of his poetry. Sir Richard Jebb, who was peculiarly qualified to appreciate his art, has admirably pointed the contrast between Sophocles and his predecessor: "Aeschylus," he says, "was a great creator; Sophocles pre-eminently a great artist. He took the legends, and presented them in a harmonious and beautiful form, suitable to the material, and intelligible to all men."

This does not mean that Aeschylus was not an artist: nor does it imply that Sophocles lacked originality. The Attic genius is less remarkable for creation than for its power of giving new and continually more perfect expression to old ideas. Aeschylus, though, like all Greek artists, he used old stories and ideas, and though his poems are, as I have tried to show, finely balanced compositions in which no touch is wasted, has yet a romantic imagination, a kind of religious enthusiasm, a moral fervour, which are Dorian rather than Ionian, astonishing in an Attic poet. The particular story is to him an illustration or an apparent contradiction of the moral government of the world : he modifies it that it may more clearly illustrate or less flagrantly contradict his general feeling : he makes it significant by clothing it in gorgeous language, by drawing parallels between it and other stories, by music and pageantry : always he makes the story stand for something greater than itself, and it is that greater thing which is the subject of his poem. His theme is thus the universe, and he is deeply concerned to teach something about the universe. To Sophocles the story is the thing. His aim is not to use the story as the basis of a religious poem, but to present the story itself : he accepts its morality, and uses its religious ideas : but, as Mr Mackail has well remarked, it is neither ethics nor theology that he gives us : it is "the endless wonderfulness of life." In other words he is first of all a dramatist, only secondarily a teacher or a thinker.

In that respect he is like Homer : this, not simply his vocabulary and syntax, makes him "the most Homeric" of the Attic poets. Like Homer, he impresses his own outlook on the traditional material : consciously and unconsciously he is always humanising, refining, spiritualising : but for him, as for Homer, that is not the aim. He wishes to present a vivid story of real life : the life which he would present is not the life of contemporary Athens, but the heroic age, when, as he probably believed, men had been greater in spirit, in valour and suffering and crime, when gods intervened more directly in the affairs of men. The heroes were for him, as for Homer, sons of the gods, a race apart from the men of his own days : for him, indeed, they were greater since in Greece they were worshipped as they had not been in Ionia : and the authentic record of these heroes, to be accepted without excessive scepticism, was for him the epic, the wisdom of the sages, lyric poetry and earlier tragedy. His business was to make these stories live in a new form, dramatic instead of narrative : he had to tell the tale no longer as a story-teller, who narrates, but, as a dramatist, through the speeches and the actions of the characters themselves. Here again we must remember the warning that the conventions of the Attic theatre were not our own.

The clue then to the art of Sophocles is that he tried to present the legendary event as a living reality, treating the story as a theme important for its own sake, not valuable chiefly for what it taught or suggested. Naturally, he was led to discard the connected Trilogy. Aeschylus, by his method, could show the history of a clan : he could trace the working of a curse or an hereditary taint in successive generations : for his purpose the similarity of incident in successive dramas was an advantage, because the story was in fact less important than the theme or general idea. Aristotle, on the other hand, for whom Sophocles was the model tragedian, demands that tragedy should imitate an action complete and whole and of a certain magnitude. This unity or singleness of event is indeed necessary for a perfect story, whether it be told as epic or presented as drama : what Aristotle calls the "episodic plot" is bad in a play or in a narrative poem (and, we may add, in a novel), so long as the story is the thing to which we are asked to give attention. Once more, it was because Sophocles was Homeric, that is to say *a story-teller,* that his instinct made him limit his scope and dramatise a single crisis in a single independent play.

He was of course (witness the *Oedipus Tyrannus*) a master of theatrical technique, but that, perhaps, is not his greatest merit. It is true that every detail of his plot and language contributes to the movement of the whole composition. But his genius is greater than his technique ; for he creates, as actors or sufferers in his legendary events, real living human beings. All his artistic skill, all the care which he lavishes on detail, is a means to the creation of these great men and women. That is the bent of his genius, and the natural object of his thought. It is because he is supremely interested in human beings as such that he cares to make the story, as a story, the aim and object of his art. It is indeed the condition of success in story-telling that events should be results of character.

Consciously or unconsciously, it appears, Sophocles was led by his interest in human emotions to that objective, non-moral, non-critical treatment of the myths which is on the whole characteristic of his work. He starts, no doubt, with the intention simply of presenting, in a worthy form, according to the conventions of the theatre, a piece of the heroic mythology. In presenting it, he gives it life. Each of his dramas is, essentially, the picture of a crisis in the experience and emotion of some great person.

When he is at his best, everything is subordinated to this central, personal interest. The events are so arranged that they display the central character reacting to the stress of different circumstances: conversely, granted the state of affairs which is postulated at the outset, events within the play are such as follow naturally from the characters. As in a skilful painting strands of colour lead the eye, almost unconsciously, to that which the painter

desires to emphasize, so in the drama of Sophocles
the minor characters are subtly calculated, and throw
the hero or heroine into high relief. Sometimes the
effect is made by the suggestion of a certain like-
ness or sympathy : more often contrast is employed.
Probably Sophocles was the first tragedian who
habitually used a third actor : it was in order that
he might more freely illuminate the central figure.
Each of his persons is an individual human being :
but in general each is significant chiefly in relation
to the one great person of the play. The plot is
complicated, incidents are varied, minor characters
multiplied and differentiated : but in all these devices
it is the aim of the dramatist not to dissipate but to
concentrate, not to weaken but to intensify the all-
important central personal tragedy.

Language also was pressed into the service of
character. The difficulty of the language of Aeschylus
is due partly to his imaginative fertility : instinctively
he personifies simple objects and clothes simple ideas
in metaphor : his style, moreover, is condensed and
packed with suggestions, once alive, which we can
now animate only by research. Of Sophocles, Porson
observed that his speech was sometimes *obscurior
quam par erat*, but his difficulty is different from
that of Aeschylus, and due to a different reason.
Blaydes was even more severe : "His language," he
wrote, "is often extremely harsh ; his formation of

sentences unnatural, intricate and obscure; his style
stiff and laboured; his constructions forced; his
metaphors strained...." That is the criticism of a
grammarian, not of a poet: for in fact Sophocles
provides inexhaustible material for grammatical discussion. The reason is not that his constructions
are forced, but that they are too much like human
thought to be reducible to rules. The form of the
sentences is subtly modified, not indeed to resemble
the language of the market-place, but to suggest and
ideally to reflect the subtlety of the mind. The
meaning is not obscure, though it cannot be para-
phrased. Thought and emotion are difficult enough
to convey by any language: when art has compelled
language to convey them with peculiar vividness,
when in fact a poetical phrase has been created, the
precise meaning is in the words: it *is* what the words
say, and it cannot be expressed in any other words.
That is the truth about Sophoclean language at its
best: it is hard to analyse, impossible to translate:
but it is intensely alive. The subtle variations are
often, no doubt, intended (like the subtleties of
Virgil) to heighten the beauty or the rhetorical
point of the sentence; but in general they actually
make the language not less but more dramatic, not·
less but more expressive of the thought of the
speaker. The style is to the speech of ordinary men
as the characters are to characters of ordinary life.

I have tried, for clearness, to suggest at the outset the nature of the work and the tendency of the genius of Sophocles. His work was to vivify the traditional story in the new, dramatic, form : his tendency was to vivify it by selecting a portion of the story which contained a moral or emotional crisis, to make that portion the subject of a harmoniously constructed drama, and to use all the resources of his art in order to heighten the reality of the dominant heroic character whose crisis is the theme. That is, I believe, the direction in which his greatness lies. But, if this general view is admitted, it becomes ridiculous to assert that his achievement was perfect, his art without flaw. Just as the assertion that he "saw life steadily and saw it whole" challenges criticism, and may draw us from his real greatness into irrelevant discussion of his "conventional idealism" or his "bluntness of moral perception"; so the assertion that his art is "impeccable" may rob us of delight and lead us to the grievous error of supposing that his art was, is, and must be unpopular. Great as the achievement is, it is not perfect; and its faults are due to the intractable nature of the conventions and the material which the dramatist had to use.

Consider first the conventions, modified, yet not entirely harmonised with the dramatic purpose. "The drama," in the words of Burke, "was not yet

brought to perfection ; and like those animals which
change their state, some parts of the old narrative
still adhered. It still had a chorus, it still had a
prologue to explain the design ; and the perfect
Drama, an automaton supported and moved without
any foreign help, was formed late and gradually."
The narrative element, the long speeches of mes-
sengers in which so much of the action is related
not enacted, need not trouble us : Sophocles has
made this element as vivid as can be desired. The
prologue, moreover, he has successfully subdued to
his dramatic purpose, though it must be admitted
that the past history and the situation which has
to be assumed at the outset is generally more complicated than would be tolerable in a modern play.
But the chorus, though it is not ever irrelevant, and
though it has suffered an artistic change, is generally
not essential to the main dramatic end. It is used
indeed with consummate skill to accompany, express,
and heighten the emotional phases through which
the drama moves : by its sympathy or its failure
to understand it is kept within the drama, and it
actually helps the drama when it throws into relief
the central character. But that is not enough. Its
beauty is its own. However skilfully it is saved from
irrelevance, however much it is made to add to the
significance of the whole, it remains essentially undramatic, a charming and appropriate ornament, but

still an ornament, not an indispensable part of the play. Without its lyrics an Aeschylean drama ceases to be what it is : a Sophoclean play loses a grace (for Sophocles is not only a dramatist but also an exquisite maker of lyric), but it remains what it is, essentially great drama, and the grace which it loses is really an additional and alien grace.

The difficulty inherent in the material is less obvious, but it exists. It is a common fault in writers of Chronicle plays, and of what are called Historical or Realistic dramas, to introduce historical or actual details improper to their design : they are persuaded that, in spite of Aristotle, all that is true historically is also possible dramatically. But Aristotle was right, as well as witty, when he said : "There is no reason why *some* events that have actually happened should not conform to the law of the probable and possible." The danger of false realism was diminished for the Greeks by the fact that their materials were heroic, legendary, already made poetically probable. They were fluid and could be adapted, within certain limits, by the poet. But there were certain limits, not less real because they were not fixed. Though Sophocles in general moves freely and creates his new life in the ancient framework easily enough, yet he is sometimes thrown out, obliged to modify his poetical design, in order to

SH.   7 preserve the outline of the mythical event. "It is not," to quote Burke again, "the incompatibility or agreeableness of incidents, characters, or sentiments with the probable in fact, but with propriety in design, that admits or excludes them from a place in any composition. We may as well urge that stones, sand, clay, and metals, lie in a certain manner in the earth, as a reason for building with these materials, and in that manner, as for writing according to the accidental disposition of characters in Nature." Mythology, like Nature, has accidental dispositions. An Athenian poet who treats of Electra, however he may concentrate the interest on his heroine, must, when the crisis comes, give chief place to Orestes the Deliverer.

The fact that the material is traditional imposes, then, certain restrictions on the freedom of plot and character. But there are compensations not to be despised. The stories, characters, even the poetical phrases of these tragedies came to the ancient audience with associations now lost beyond recovery. As a musician is delighted when he hears in some new symphony quotations from an older work, allusions to familiar themes, so the Athenian listeners must have responded to delicate touches, happy reminiscences. The *Electra*, which we can partly appreciate from this point of view, is full of new and delightful modifications of old themes from the *Libation-Pourers.* For those who can remember how the return of Orestes in the Aeschylean drama is compared, with language drawn from the Mysteries, to the shining of a light in darkness, there is a double beauty in the prologue, when the faithful servant shows the exile his home, and bids him act.

"Since now at last the clear shining of the sun wakes to song for us the morning voices of birds, and the black night of stars is over." The same note sounds again in the first words of Electra, "O holy light!" Or if we turn to the crisis of the vengeance, there also slight sure touches recall the motives which reverberate so terribly throughout the Aeschylean trilogy. The ancient riches of the house, the old blood feud, the living spirit of the murdered father— "champion of the nether powers, with feet of guile" —are all on the lips of the chorus, when Orestes and Pylades, "the hounds that run in the track of crime, not to be escaped, have passed beneath the palace roof" to slay the sinners: and as the Aeschylean Orestes called in his first words upon Hermes of the Nether World to be his saviour and fellow-fighter, so now the chorus cry that Hermes son of Maia, who is god of trickery as well as guardian of the dead, "has kept the plot from discovery, and now leads on the avengers." Electra issues from the palace, and bids the chorus "Wait in silence, for the deed is being done." Then, when they ask her to describe the scene within, she answers: "The woman is preparing the urn for burial, and the two avengers stand by her ready." The words are dramatic enough, for the urn which Clytaemnestra is preparing contains, she thinks, the ashes of her son, who is ready, living, to slay her: but there is more than that: it is fitting that when death takes her she should be busy with a *Lebes* (urn or cauldron), for we have not forgotten "the tale of a cauldron's murderous treachery," the "silvern coffer" wherein Agamemnon lay, the fatal bath with which she comforted her lord. (See e.g. *Agam.* 1120, 1540; *Cho.* 489, 666, 1070; *Eum.* 464, 636). The double cry of the dying woman is the cry which thrilled the spectator of the *Agamemnon.* When Aegisthus, triumphant in the reported death of the avenger, has drawn the covering from the body which he thinks is that of Orestes, he is for a moment dazed: he does not realise that it is Clytaemnestra who is dead: but he asks a question full of meaning to the audience: "In what men's net was this victim trapped?" It is a slight allusion, but poignant enough, to the motive of the net or web which was the key-note of such great imaginative poetry in the trilogy: whether, to make the scene more perfect, Clytaemnestra lay wrapped in the fatal purple, we do not know.

Old incidents of plot as well as ideas are taken and adapted to new purposes. On that subject we cannot now insist: any reader can trace for himself the finer dramatic economy with which Sophocles has treated the lock of hair offered by Orestes at his father's tomb, and the ruse by which the avenger gains admission to the palace. It will be observed that in spite of old themes and motives the drama is a new creation: for everything here is calculated to heighten the interest of Electra. To that end the mother-murder is made less significant: Aegisthus has become, as in the Homeric story, the chief criminal: the murder of Clytaemnestra is a just, not questionable act of vengeance: Apollo was consulted not as to the righteousness of the deed, but as to the best means for its accomplishment: Orestes slays her, and the immediate thought of Electra is the hope that Aegisthus may suffer the like fate. So much has Electra become the central figure that Orestes, when he tells her Clytaemnestra is dead, can say: "Fear no more: your mother will not do you wrong again." The fact that Orestes is the avenger has already been cited as a discrepancy between the design of Sophocles and his material: the discrepancy is triumphantly obscured. For the predominant passion which makes Electra great is not the passion for vengeance: it is the love of her dead father. When Agamemnon was murdered, she

was old enough to understand: she saved Orestes and
loved him as her father's future avenger: she hates
Aegisthus and her mother for their hatred of Agamemnon: she cares little for the weak and charming
Chrysothemis, because her love for Agamemnon is
not great enough: after the numb despair which
follows the news of the avenger's death, she rises
to the height of tragic determination: herself, though
she will certainly die for it, she will slay the usurpers.
At that moment Sophocles has conquered, so far as it
was possible to conquer, the legend which left her
inactive.   Finally, when Orestes appears alive, she
welcomes him in a passion of joy and love, as the
incarnation of her father who is still first in her
thought.   The chorus and Chrysothemis blame her
stubborn loyalty, and modern critics generally agree
with them; but it is difficult to believe that Sophocles
would have agreed.

Not only was Sophocles dealing with traditional
material, but also the audience and probably the poet
still believed in the potency of heroes and still made
offerings at their graves. The motives and machinery
of Sophoclean tragedy are mainly human, but much
will be puzzling if we forget that the characters were
still supposed to influence the fortunes of the Athenian
state. Ajax, the Salaminian hero, had become one of
the guardians of Athens when his native island became

Athenian, and he helped to win the battle of Salamis.
Herodotus, the friend and younger contemporary of
Sophocles, displays no doubt on that: he records
with due solemnity that before the battle Ajax and
his father Telamon were summoned from Salamis
to aid the Greeks, and a ship was sent to Aegina to
fetch Aeacus and the other Aeacids. It is the fact
that Ajax meant so much to Athens, not simply the
importance attached by Athenians to burial in general,
that explains why, when to our minds the tragedy of
Ajax has nobly culminated in his death, the play of
Sophocles goes on through weary tracts of argument
about his burying. Ajax had been adjudged less
worthy than Odysseus to receive the weapons of
Achilles, the guerdon of the bravest Greeks at Troy;
he had plotted against his own leaders; had been
smitten, to his shame, with a divine madness; had
been the laughing-stock of his enemies; had fallen
by his own hand. The honour of such a hero was
a delicate matter. Pindar, most courtly of flatterers,
had to tread lightly here. So Sophocles, though the
part of the play which is of permanent value is the
human story of a wounded pride that could find no
cure save in self-destruction, was obliged to show how
the dishonoured hero was reinstated, and honoured
even by his enemies, after death. The action is complete when Ajax falls upon his sword; but the subject,
the justification and the glorifying of the hero, passes,

as M. Allègre has remarked, beyond the limits of the
action. The same critic has analysed the skilful composition by which the suicide and the panegyric are
made into one poem. Dramatically wounded honour,
a purely human motive, is enough to cause the suicide;
yet the death, though Ajax is a human being acting
freely without supernatural impulsion, is in fact a
judgment of divine wrath against *Hybris* [῞Υβρις].
Athene, the goddess of Athens, punishes the arrogance
of this Athenian hero; but, in the sequel, the generals,
the sons of Atreus, are arrogant, commit *Hybris*, in
their treatment of their fallen enemy, and finally it
is by the intercession of Odysseus, the favourite of
Athene, the man whom Ajax in his madness loathed
and insulted and would have killed, that the
generals are turned from their *Hybris* and the hero
is accorded the due honours of the grave. Skilful
as all this is, sufficient to make the whole intensely
moving to the audience, it remains true that the
drama is not a perfect work of art: Sophocles
is so great that we need not labour to prove him
impeccable.

Of the *Oedipus at Colonus* Sir Richard Jebb
observed: "It is a patriotic play, intensely Attic in
feeling, with scarcely any plot, but of the highest
interest and charm: the passing of Oedipus at the
sacred Colonus is of a sublime beauty." That is
an admirable summary, of course; yet for an ancient

spectator there was a plot, and an exciting plot. He saw not only the interests of Oedipus but also the welfare of Attica at stake. We understand the mystical beauty of the hero's end: Oedipus, polluted by great evils (evils done unwittingly, yet not less carrying pollution) is at length purified by suffering, received by the Kindly Goddesses of the under-world at Colonus, welcomed by the piety of the Athenian hero-king, acknowledged by the thunder of Olympian Zeus, and finally, by the perfect harmony of the divine will with his own, he is given rest. But the wrangling with the Theban kinsmen who desire to secure the person of the exile; the terrible curse which Oedipus pronounces on his sons: these things are also part of the drama. We may say that these incidents are put into the play because they are part of the Oedipus legend; that is partly true. We may say that they serve to show that the old fire burns still in the heart of the suffering but unconquered hero; and that is also true. But these scenes are more than pieces of conventional padding, or rather awkward touches of characterisation; they are essential to the plot. To an Athenian it is important not only that Oedipus should find rest, but that his rest should be in Attica. For the grave of Oedipus, who slept at Colonus, was believed to be "for the weal of the living." When pious Theseus welcomes a suppliant whom any but an Athenian would wantonly reject as evil and polluted, he is not merely illustrating Athenian virtue, but securing, though at first he does not know it, a perpetual defence for the Athenian state. When Oedipus detects the Theban designs and curses his unnatural sons, he is cursing the enemies of Athens. So long as Oedipus slept at Colonus, no invader of the Theban stock could with impunity set foot on Attic soil. As Oedipus needs Athens, so Athens needs Oedipus. That is the key to the plot. The drama is said to have been composed at the end of the poet's life; it was probably first acted some years after his death. It was composed during the last struggles of the war: before it was acted Athens had been captured. In those days the countrymen of Oedipus pressed for the destruction of the city, and she escaped not through the bones of Oedipus, but through the magnanimity of her Spartan conqueror.

The *Women of Trachis* is of the seven surviving plays the least satisfactory to modern readers. Its weakness may serve to illustrate the peculiar difficulty with which Sophocles had always to deal. The theme is the divinely ordered issue of the destiny of Heracles, the Dorian Hero, whose labours ended only with his life: the action shows the working out of the divine will and the accomplishment of ancient oracles by the destruction of the hero through the hate of his dead enemy Nessus: the instrument of that hate is

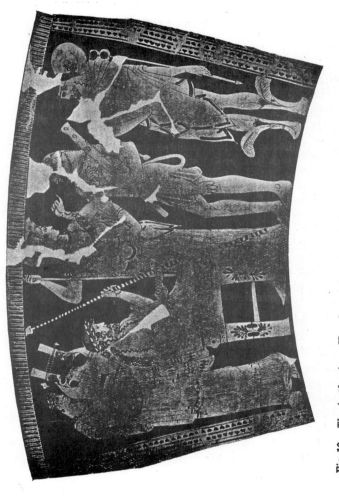

Fig. 10. *The Apotheosis of Heracles.* Athene introduces the deified hero to Zeus, and Hermes, as the messenger of the gods, assists at the ceremony. Notice the lion's skin and club of Heracles, and the winged boots, the wand and travelling-hat of Hermes.

the unwitting Deianeira. Now Sophocles, following
his natural tendency, creates in Deianeira a living
person: so successful is the creation that Deianeira
concerns us even more than Heracles. There is, in
fact, a tragedy within a tragedy: the human tragedy
naturally interests the modern reader more than the
heroic—"Deianeira has an imperishable charm:
Heracles, when he appears in the third part of the
play, is less effective."

Probably this distraction of sympathy was less
apparent to the ancient audience than it is to us.
They started, of course, with a prejudice in favour
of Heracles. They knew him already as the typical
virtuous man, destroyer of monsters, civiliser of the
world; as for his vices ("diseases," the Greeks would
have called them),—his love of food and wine and
wenches—his sainthood was not the less but rather
the more popular for all that. The son of Zeus by
a mortal woman, he had been received after death
into the ranks of the Olympians. His reception in
Olympia and his introduction to the divine company
by Athene is a favourite theme of Attic vase-painters
(cf. fig. 10). Sophocles, indeed, says nothing of the
apotheosis; but the double aspect of Heracles, worshipped both as a god and as a hero, must be
remembered when we try to imagine the effect of
the play. In life his destiny had been to suffer
for the sake of man; his strength was invincible,

like that of Samson, and, like Samson, he was conquered by one thing only, namely the love of women. He conquered all else: his own lust he could not conquer. From this point of view my friend Mr A. Y. Campbell has expounded the play in an essay, soon, I hope, to be published. He has shown how Sophocles

Fig. 11. The Fight of Heracles (with lion-skin and club, cf. fig. 10) and the River-God Achelous. Deianeira in the background is shown by her lotus-sceptre to be a princess.

has introduced monstrous shapes, half-bestial, half-human, as recurring symbols of lust. Heracles had won Deianeira as his bride by rescuing her from a brutal suitor, the river-god Achelous who came in three shapes as wooer, "now as a bull, now as a serpent with sheeny coils, now with trunk of man and front of ox, while from a shaggy beard the streams of fountain-water flowed abroad" (cf. fig. 11). Nessus, the Centaur, was another such lustful monster: when Heracles and his new bride were fording a river, the Centaur offered violence to Deianeira, and for that he was killed by Heracles. Before he died he gave to Deianeira an ointment, the poisoned blood of Cheiron, bidding her keep it safely since it would be a sure love-charm to bring back Heracles if ever he proved unfaithful. She took it and remembered, thinking no evil. All that happened long before the opening of the drama, but is of vital importance to the action.

The time has come at which, according to oracles, the hero will accomplish his last labour and achieve rest or death. He has been absent for fifteen months and no news of him has come to his wife. He has, though she does not yet know it, been suffering the worst of degradations: the strong Greek has been in bondage, spinning wool like a slave-girl for an oriental mistress. Released from that service, he is now besieging Oechalia—the cause again a woman, Iole, to gain whose person he destroys her city. In the moment of his triumph, to win back his love, Deianeira sends him the fatal robe, anointed with the gift of Nessus. Heracles, therefore, who twice saved Deianeira from bestial lust, is himself

struck down by the hate of the beast whom he slew,
at the moment when he has lately fallen twice a
victim to his own unbridled lust. When he first
realises that the gift of his wife is poisoned with a
fiery venom which eats into his flesh, he naturally
supposes that she is jealous and murderous. The
words of his son reveal to him the truth: the am-
biguous oracles foretold not rest but death. In
that moment for the audience and for Sophocles
the destiny of Heracles is of more account than the
death of Deianeira. It is the working of the divine
will through Nessus and through Deianeira that
becomes significant. That is why we hear no self-
reproaches from the hero. In this crisis he realises
the meaning of all his life: in accordance with
the oracles of the gods he gives orders for his
solemn burning on the mountain-top, on a pyre
kindled by the hand of his own son. To us this
conclusion may seem heartless: to the audience
for whom Heracles was the hero, Deianeira only an
incident, and a fatal incident, in his life, it is simply
appropriate.

As for Deianeira, it is at least questionable
whether she was meant to seem so heroic as to
modern sentiment she certainly appears, though her
faithfulness and gentleness were, no doubt, intended to heighten the tragedy. She is sometimes blamed by modern critics for her credulity in

accepting and using the gift of Nessus; but that is hardly just. Until the gift is sent to Heracles she is the victim of a supernatural delusion: the hate of Nessus has power to blind her to the nature of his gift. French critics, moreover, have found her patience somewhat irritating: "jealousy," they say, "must either blaze into revengefulness or die." Deianeira is, they think, too gentle to be human. Sophocles was deliberately robbing Deianeira of personality in order to make it clear that the tragedy was the result of superhuman agency. That is certainly not the impression of English readers, who readily accept the Gilbertian view of woman's love, "everything for him, nothing at all for her." And for all its sentimental exaggeration, I think the English view is nearer the truth. Sophocles was really seized by the pathos of her situation, sympathised with her wrongs, painted a character more lovable than strong, yet so lovable that her weakness seems comparatively unimportant. But for a Greek audience he could paint such a character without fear that the balance of his play would be destroyed.

Her weakness made her sin. She used a love-charm; and witchcraft, even for good ends, is intolerable where its possible efficacy is believed. Her just pity for Iole astonishes us, and is one of the noblest touches in Greek tragedy; yet to the audience it must have been less astonishing than it is to us. For the gross cruelty of Heracles in bringing home a concubine was also to them less astonishing. In the fourth century an orator could say to an Athenian jury: "We use harlots for our pleasure; concubines we use to serve our comfort, and wives for the begetting of children." Respectable citizens in the audience may themselves have had concubines as well as lawful wives: the life of Sophocles himself will illustrate my point. To such men Deianeira may have seemed to have behaved well, as a noble woman should: an ordinary woman might have shown jealousy and taken some wild vengeance on the concubine: Deianeira was not, indeed, like Clytaemnestra, with whom she was pointedly contrasted by the construction of the play. Even so her nobility can hardly have impressed a Greek as it impresses us. To Sophocles, though Heracles sinned, his sin was venial; though Deianeira was a good and patient wife, she was hardly sublime.

Yet it would be unfair to leave the play with this remark. The mere representation of Deianeira, the truth and sympathy of the painting, are the sign that Sophocles, unconsciously or consciously, transcends the limits of the conventional attitude. So in general his humanity transcends and transfigures the superstition and immorality of his traditional material.

There remain three dramas whose greatness

SH. 8

requires little commentary; *Antigone, Oedipus Tyrannus, Philoctetes.*

The first well illustrates the danger of approaching a Greek drama with preconceived and arbitrary notions of the nature of Tragedy. Hegel's theory that Tragedy involves a clashing and a reconciliation of two principles, both of which are somehow right, and Aristotle's notion that the hero of a tragedy must be imperfect lest the catastrophe shock the moral sense, have combined to obscure the meaning of this drama. Antigone, we are told, represents the family or the individual conscience set in tragic conflict with Creon as the representative of the state or law. Now it is true that in the time of Sophocles, when Athenian intelligence, stimulated by many influences, was examining the bases of morality, the idea of obedience to the law as law was seen by many people to be morally unsatisfying: gradually the idea of individual right and duty was distinguished, and supplanted the old notion of uncritical obedience to the custom of one's city. This contrast between local practice and the universal, divine, unwritten law of righteousness is certainly reflected in the play. The main idea, however, is not a conflict between law and conscience, family and state, but rather a heroic sacrifice of life, and of a happy life, to pious duty and the love of a dead brother. Creon is not the representative of law, although he arrogates the right to dictate it. In Aeschylus the decree that Polyneices should lie unburied was a decree of the state: doubtless, in the old tradition, it was a tolerable act of retribution that the state should leave a traitor's body unburied. In Sophocles the decree is impious. Men still believed that lack of burial was a terrible evil to the dead; but the feeling, already expressed in Homer, that it is not good to persecute a fallen enemy, had by this time become so strong that to an Athenian audience Creon's edict must at once have stamped him as a wicked and foolhardy man. The plague that resulted is sufficient proof of that. He is in fact a tyrant, suspicious, fearful of popular opposition, obstinate, arrogant, breaking out, when he is thwarted, into blasphemy. His ruin is the punishment of his impiety, though it is dramatically the result of his death-sentence on Antigone, which, too late, he has endeavoured to recall.

On the other hand, as the blasphemy of Creon has been forgotten in the desire to make him represent the law, so a fault has been found in Antigone to make her fate seem somehow just. She is devoted to her brother and will bury him though she die for it: that is right. But she is "too provocative," she is "excessive in her zeal." The chorus in fact are right and she is so far wrong. The point is arguable, but I believe the chorus are not right: they seem to me to be used, like Ismene, dramatically to heighten

n and heroism. Of course she has
: that is simply good psychology.
for her family is always hard: so
_ ___g for an idea. Her love is concentrated on one person, her one idea absorbs her.
When there is no further need for action, her passion
leaves her weak. It is good psychology again which
makes her grieve for the happiness which she must
lose, and argue with herself to justify her choice in
terms that sound as frigid as her earlier defiance was
passionate. The point of the play is therefore simpler
and nobler than any conflict between two duties.
Antigone, in a situation which meant death or the
betrayal of her noblest instinct, chose death and
made the better choice: Creon, who loved power
more than righteousness, was smitten through the
woman whose powerlessness he had wronged, and so
learned righteousness through suffering.

Similarly in the *Oedipus Tyrannus* the passionate
self-confidence of Oedipus heightens, but is not intended to "justify" his tragedy. At the outset he
seems of all men farthest removed from evil, a
great king, honoured by his people, and approached
by them almost as a god in their trouble. The
drama (which in strength and variety, in concen-
tration of interest, in the movement of events, the
greatness of the central figure, and the splendid
shock of the catastrophe, is the noblest work of

Sophocles) consists of a chain of incidents, naturally connected, tending to increase the confidence of the king and to scatter even shadows of conceivable danger. The whole is dominated by the will of Oedipus, who insists on dragging truth to light. Throughout, as the spectator perceives, the king is drawing nearer to a terrible discovery, that he, the saviour of the city, is of all men most wretched, most polluted. We are not to look for poetic justice here: the point is not that Oedipus is a sinner righteously punished. Nor must we try to justify or to indict the gods whose will is thus accomplished. Oedipus is a great man, greatly ruined. His fate is like human life, terrible, capable of being greatest when it is most terrible; it is meant to make us feel the greatness, not the goodness or badness, of the world in which such events may happen.

Finally the *Philoctetes* is perhaps the best example of the Sophoclean power of making human beings live. Its interest is hardly tragic, for the hero, in spite of the title, is a fortunate and brilliant youth, Neoptolemus, the son of Achilles. An oracle declared that without the aid of Neoptolemus and without the bow of Philoctetes Troy could not be captured by the Greeks. But Philoctetes hated the Greeks for a great wrong. When first they were sailing for Troy, he had been bitten by a poisonous serpent, and they had abandoned him on a desolate island in disgust and

superstitious horror at his wound. His bow at length
became necessary for their success, but his hatred
made a reconciliation seem impossible. He must
be trapped by guile. Odysseus, his ancient enemy,
the most cunning of the Greeks, undertook the task
of stealing his weapon, and, to entrap the hero, employed young Neoptolemus, lately arrived at Troy.
When the drama opens, Neoptolemus and Odysseus
have just landed on the island, and in the first scene
the youth is informed of the deceit which he must
practise. The plot fails. At the end Philoctetes has
possession of his bow, and is no nearer than before to
reconciliation.   A divine apparition, Heracles, the
old companion of Philoctetes and the ancient master
of the bow, satisfactorily ends the story in accordance
with the legendary fact. Philoctetes and Neoptolemus
at his command set out for Troy to accomplish their
destined exploit.

Ostensibly therefore Philoctetes is the central
figure, and the subject a human plot which failed,
whose object was, however, accomplished through a
quite arbitrary divine intervention. From that point
of view critics have been distressed by the epilogue,
and have even sometimes suggested that it would
have been better had Philoctetes been represented
as touched by the generosity of Neoptolemus, and
so moved to reconciliation with the Greeks. The
suggestion is not happy: it ignores the fact that

though ostensibly Philoctetes is the subject, dramatic
interest centres on Neoptolemus. The unaltered hate
of Philoctetes for the Greeks is essential to the play.
Had he abandoned it under any impulse less cogent,
less mechanical than a divine command, the plot would
have been duplicated and the interest weakened. The
perfect Sophoclean drama represents a revolution in
one character, not in two. Philoctetes is pathetic

Fig. 12. Philoctetes: in his right
hand he holds the wing of a
bird with which he fans his
wounded leg, in his left hand
is the bow.

through his situation and his physical suffering: he
is still humane and noble in his misery: his hatred of
the Greeks is just: his confidence in Neoptolemus
and his love for the youth whom he regards as his
deliverer are generous: but Neoptolemus, not Philoctetes, is the hero. The oracle, the plot, the character
of Philoctetes, are created or manipulated for the sake

of Neoptolemus. The question whether the bow will be secured concerns us chiefly because without it Neoptolemus will not have the glory of the capture of Troy. The subject is an ingenuous youth, son of a magnanimous father, urged by apparent duty and by desire of glory to an action which instinctively he hates as dishonourable. The desire of reputation may or may not have been more powerful in ancient Greece than it is to-day: certainly the Athenians were more frank than modern Englishmen in acknowledging it. Anyhow, the glory which depends for Neoptolemus on the stealing of the bow is great enough at first to overcome his scruples, probably great enough to justify his conduct to the audience. But the suffering, the dignity, the confidence of Philoctetes work a change in the youth for which *conversion* is the obvious name. To all intents and purposes he succeeds in trapping Philoctetes; then, of his own will, he breaks obedience to Odysseus, undeceives his victim, gives him back the weapon which makes him master of his fate, and actually turns away from Troy and surrenders his prospect of glory by consenting to carry Philoctetes with him back to Greece. Thus the sacrifice of Neoptolemus is the theme, and the human drama, though it is finally harmonised with the divinely-appointed destiny of Philoctetes and of Troy, is in fact free and completely victorious.

I have not attempted to summarise the religious and moral teaching which are implied in these dramas: nor have I discussed at length the treatment of plot and chorus or the characteristic use of what is called "tragic irony." In all these spheres Sophocles is great, but his greatest gift to literature is the representation of human nobility. The passionate devotion of Antigone, the dogged love of Electra, the imperious will of Oedipus, the gentleness of Deianeira, the generosity of Neoptolemus, the wounded honour of Ajax—these are his great achievement, and it is on this achievement that ·I have endeavoured to lay stress.

CHAPTER V

EURIPIDES.

THE Athens of Pericles was the parent of another Athens less harmonious but not less great. Pericles, according to the Funeral Oration, found in his city the perfect marriage of reflectiveness and action, of art and simplicity, of philosophy and sense. Sophocles and Pheidias appeared to celebrate a religion free of superstition, and a spirit of enquiry neither flippant nor insane. In the *salon* of Aspasia, pious, austere and dignified Athenians may have listened to old Damon expounding the principles of music; to Zeno putting logical dilemmas; to Anaxagoras explaining how the world is a cosmos created by divine intelligence, the *Nous*; or to Protagoras discussing with his host the interminable problem of the theory of punishment, perhaps suggesting as a commonsense hypothesis that "the individual is the measure of truth." It may well have seemed that the age of reasonable freedom had come. Nor are we to suppose that Pericles or his friends were insincere when, from such discussions, they passed to the worship of the gods. Ritual meant more than dogma in the pagan cults : we know of nothing in the speculations of Anaxagoras which need have prevented him from honouring the Zeus whose image Pheidias created, and the logic of Zeno was devised for the defence of a doctrine easily reconciled with the practice of the ordinary cults. Though immoral inferences were to be drawn from the hypothesis of Protagoras, they were assuredly not drawn by the respectable moralist himself.

Superstition, however, still prevailed among the mass of citizens. Damon was thought dangerous and driven into exile. Anaxagoras, as his opinions became known, was suspected of impiety, and, just before the death of Pericles, was tried and banished. ·Later, Protagoras, for an expression of what has been called "a cautious agnosticism," was threatened with prosecution, fled from Athens, and is said to have been drowned on his voyage. His books were publicly burnt. Nor is all this surprising. For, in fact, if the sun is an incandescent rock, as Anaxagoras supposed, and no divinity, there is danger also for Zeus the Thunderer. If man is the measure of all things, the sacrilegious traitor is no worse than the pious citizen. So long, moreover, as morality meant duty to the state, and the state depended on Olympians, cruel,

jealous, lustful, capricious, so long must a moral
reformer question the very basis of morality ; and so
long must such a questioner, though he were as pious
as Socrates, be thought a danger and a perverter of
the young.   So Socrates was put to death.

Superstition still prevailed. Therefore the Enlightenment was salutary, and was necessarily dis-
ruptive.   It was also inevitable.   When the fathers
think the Age of Reason is achieved, the sons may be
trusted, if they are of a good stock, to see that it
is still far off.   The revolution in thought, which
Aristophanes deplored, was the legitimate offspring
of the Periclean age, though like most children it
scandalised its parent. From the time when Pericles
became supreme, Athens was the centre of Greece
Her citizens travelled, and saw the customs of many
nations.   In the assembly and the law-courts they
needed the arts of rhetoric, even before teachers
came from Sicily to teach them argument.   All men
who had ideas found listeners and ready talkers in
Athenian gymnasia, and the seeds of opinion ripened
after the sowers had perhaps been sent about their
business.   Everything, divine and human, had to
stand the test of criticism. Women presumed, or
some men on behalf of them presumed, to protest
against the social system which made the strange
position of Aspasia possible.   It was even suggested
that barbarians or slaves might sometimes be as

good as Greeks and citizens. Nobler spirits sought
a sanction for morality in human feeling and good
sense, but of course there were baser men to whom
enlightenment meant nothing but the breaking of
old sanctions. Some held, a few professed, probably
some also put into practice, the doctrine that justice
is no more than the rule of the strong. Pericles
had spoken of wisdom joined with manliness, and
of reflection that did not hinder action: in a few
years after his death, the manly cry of Cleon urging
a massacre was heard—"Act now: delay is fatal:
reflection will unman you." To some it seemed that
politics had become a questionable business, that a
man should find out what was good before he tried
to guide his fellows, that the pursuit of truth was
nobler than the service of a city. Yet all the while,
this city was fighting the war which was to end in
the destruction of her material supremacy, in which
her territory was ravaged, her citizens swept away
by plague, whole armies cut to pieces. It is an
absorbing spectacle. Hardly a question that interests
us was not in some form asked by this astonishing
people. And the plays of Euripides are the mirror
of it all.

Sophocles survived him and put the chorus at the
Dionysia into mourning for him, yet the difference in
their age is not without significance. The boyhood
of Sophocles was spent in the old Athens which the

Persians destroyed. Euripides, according to the
pleasant legend, was born in Salamis on the day
of victory. He was a boy when Sophocles produced
his earliest tragedies, for it was thirteen years later
that he first as a young man competed in the festival.
By that time Pericles was already the acknowledged leader of the victorious democrats. Still,
the difference of temperament was probably more
important than this difference of age. Had Sophocles
been as young in years as Euripides he would still
have been the spiritual contemporary of Pericles and
Pheidias. But Euripides, had he been born as early
as Sophocles, could hardly have been in old age the
poet of the younger generation. As it was, he was
probably one of the first to sympathise with the new
movement, and to the end of his life (witness the
Bacchants) he retained his power of absorbing new
ideas.

He is represented as the poet of ideas in ancient
stories of his life. Aloof from affairs, melancholy,
even morose, he is contrasted with the genial and
versatile Sophocles. Observing the life in which he
took no active part, immersed in conversation or
in books,—for he possessed the rare luxury of a
library—or meditating in a cave that opened towards
Salamis, he gathered matter for the tragedies that
shocked old age and puzzled simple minds and made
the young exult and think and chatter. The attacks

of Aristophanes are the measure of his popularity
and also of the consternation which he caused. His
powers were acknowledged even by those who were
most alien from his spirit. Not only Aristophanes,
whose hostility is discounted by his rôle as carica-
turist, but also the whole audience of Aristophanes,
must have been steeped in his poetry in order to
appreciate the satire. But he was unpopular with
many of those who were compelled to admire. In
the disasters of the war those who had listened
eagerly to some new doctrine might in a few hours
turn against the teacher in a superstitious panic,
attribute some misfortune to the anger of the gods,
and demand that the impiety be driven from the
city. Euripides on his side seems to have been
oppressed by the war and by the temper of his fellow
citizens. In his last years he lived in voluntary
exile, and he died in Macedonia at the court of
Archelaus.

To a modern reader, his plays are likely to appear
at first sight ill-constructed, platitudinous, dull. The
beauty of Professor Murray's translation seems to
contradict that view, but it must be confessed that
(if we except the lyrics and some isolated passages
of dialogue) it is difficult to find in Euripides the
romantic grace which gives to that translation its
peculiar charm. Even with the aid of Professor

Murray's genius we shall probably admit that much of the original still leaves us cold. Happily the work of Dr Verrall is well known, and, whether we agree with his conclusions or not, we shall not readily reject his doctrine that the fault is more probably in us than in the author. We shall at least make some effort to understand the reason which gave these dramas such a vogue in Athens.

Perhaps the best introduction is the brilliant comedy in which Euripides was represented as contending for the post of tragic laureate to the underworld. The *Frogs* of Aristophanes was produced soon after the death of Euripides and almost immediately after that of Sophocles. Athens had now entered on the last phase of the war. Many of her allies had deserted : her coinage had been debased, her food supplies in large measure cut off: many citizens were suspected, not without reason, of treachery, many were disfranchised, some, and among them Alcibiades, in exile. There can have been few men in the audience who had not lost a father or a brother by plague or battle or the hemlock : many of them were to be among the prisoners whom Lysander slaughtered after Aegospotami: none, except the traitors, can have expected that if Athens yielded he would himself be spared. In these circumstances Aristophanes made an appeal for the abandonment of rationalism, that is to say of impious sophistry, and for a return to safe and simple piety. The appeal is interwoven with a plea for political generosity, especially for the recall of Alcibiades. The chorus of the happy Initiates is thus not only beautiful in itself, but also vitally connected with the drama. As they weave their dances in the sunlit meadows of Persephone ; as they sing their processional to Iacchus and the Ladies of Eleusis, mingling, in their good pagan fashion, piety and jest ; they remind the audience of Alcibiades, once led astray by sophistry, once the enemy of the Eleusinian goddesses, but received back, as all men knew, into their favour when, in spite of the invader, he had led down their procession to Eleusis. They point, at the same time, the contrast between Aeschylus, the poet of religion, and Euripides, the poet of persuasion, reason, argument.

We must remember this political purpose, nor must we forget that we are dealing with a comedy. Much that has been seriously pondered by the critics is pure jesting, or a subtle playing on the theme of Alcibiades. Yet, after all deductions, there remains a serious criticism of Euripides, artistic, political and moral, as well as religious. For an Athenian indeed these things are not distinct, but interdependent. The basis of it all is the contrast between Euripides and the spirit of old piety represented by Aeschylus and the Mysteries. Much of the detail is uncertain,

but this much can safely be inferred : that to those
who agreed with Aristophanes the drama of Euripides
seemed irreligious. In the theatre whose purpose
was the celebration of the gods and heroes, it was
felt that these gods and heroes had been attacked.
Secondly, the poet was thought to have ruined his
art by his introduction of "familiar things of daily
life and common use," things artistically incongruous.
Thirdly he seemed to have destroyed its moral value
by arguing matters best left undiscussed, and by
depicting action and passions which, although they
are implied in the legends, ought not to be publicly
displayed. In a word, he had robbed tragedy of its
religion, of its beauty, of its ethical grandeur. The
effect of his plays, we gather, was not that men
marvelled and became strong, but that they went
away to argue.

If we accept the hypotheses of Aristophanes it
must be admitted that his attack is just, and many
people are inclined to agree with Jebb's reluctant
censure : "His influence on the multitude in his own
day was perhaps, on the whole, not good ; for he
blurred those Hellenic ideals which were the common
man's best without definitely replacing them." It is
an old complaint against the critical spirit, and
perhaps partly just, that it can destroy but not
replace. But it is well to remember that among
the hypotheses of Aristophanes were such ideas as

these : that it is impious to say "Either Apollo did not ravish women, or he is not a god ; for a god who does evil is no god at all," that it is immoral to suggest that a man who through insanity sheds blood does not infect the air, that it is indecent to represent upon the stage a woman in love. And it is well to remember that "the common man's best" included a narrow patriotism, a contempt for foreigners and slaves, and a belief in the right and duty of rancour and revenge, which would shock the most intolerant and irascible of modern Jingoes. Criticism which shakes superstition often seems for the moment to be shaking truth and morality : but it is never true that it destroys "the common man's best," for it sets free the human spirit, and the human spirit is better than the creeds and laws and moralities in which from time to time it finds expression.

This account of the general tendency of Euripides is confirmed by consideration of the three technical faults which most critics and, I suppose, all readers find in the dramas:—that the prologues are often undramatic and wearisome in their elaborate statement of facts; that the epilogues (whether or not the *god from the machine* appears) are careless and unconvincing; and that the chorus seems often out of place and poorly manipulated. In each case what has been said provides the explanation. Euripides, like Aeschylus, treats a story for the sake of the thoughts it suggests: but the thoughts are very different from those of Aeschylus. Like Aeschylus he faces all the moral issues; but the result again is different. Where Aeschylus sees a divine legend, conveying a moral that is wrapped in mystery, Euripides sees something simply immoral and untrue, or something that suggests the inadequacy and stupidity of current notions. Therefore when Euripides treats such a story, he presents it in a form which shows its immorality or shows the folly of the popular ideas. That form is an approximation to realism. He strips the story and the characters of mystery, and says in effect: "There! That is how it looks in the light of day. What now do you think—of the god or hero—of the legend—of your attitude to your wife or concubine—of the war—of Athens?" Of course it is not always so: his interest in the emotions, good and bad, of ordinary men makes him a realist even where he is not directly criticising: his instinct is to portray humanity as it is. In any case it is fairly clear that the audience expected in his plays some reduction of the legends to the standards and emotions of contemporary life. That fact implies all the rest. When a story is to be expounded in order to be self-exposed, or to be presented in any new and startlingly unorthodox shape, it is necessary,

if we are to catch the meaning of the author, to
have clearly in our minds the version of the tale
with which he starts. That is one reason why the
prologue is elaborate in detail. Another reason is
the fact which, more than any other, explains the
forced improbable epilogues, namely that Euripides
is in the pulpit, where at least a colour of orthodoxy
must be preserved. He often banishes the supernatural altogether from the body of his play: but he is
obliged to use heroic stories as his theme, and therefore
in the prologue and the epilogue, without much caring
for the business, rarely troubling to make it plausible,
sometimes deliberately making it ridiculous, he pours
out as much heroic as the story and the occasion
demand.

His realism again is the cause of his comparative
failure with the chorus. His lyrics are melodious
and fanciful, often not unworthy to be ranked with
those of Sophocles, and usually as relevant as his.
Yet in Sophocles the effect is felt to be in harmony
with the play because the play is a revelation of the
heroic world where choruses and masks are perfectly
natural. The more the drama approximates to
ordinary life, the more we notice the incongruity of
such things. Religion insisted that Tragedy was an
act of choral worship, and so the chorus had to stay.
Euripides felt the embarrassment of their too intimate
presence in domestic scenes and secret conspiracies.

He did not succeed in solving the problem, but the methods he adopted are instructive. Sometimes he makes the chorus seem for a time realistic. Examples are the entry of Athenian maidens in the *Ion* and the visit of inquisitive women to the camp in the *Iphigeneia at Aulis*. The former is a masterpiece of its kind: the serving-maids are visiting Delphi for the first time, and are pleased above all to notice what reminds them of home: their natural comments are in spirit like the famous conversation of the Syracusan ladies in Theocritus. But it is, of course, only for a few moments and in isolated scenes that a group of fifteen persons can be made so realistic and convincing as that. So other methods are employed. The chorus holds lyrical dialogue with the leader, sections converse with one another or with the leader or with an actor, probably in excited passages individuals speak for themselves. These devices are not new: in the *Suppliants* of Aeschylus we noticed lyrical dialogue. Still this turning of the ode into a half-dramatic *scena* is one of the means by which Euripides tries to make the incongruous chorus plausible. An example is the entry of the chorus in the *Electra*, where instead of the ode we have only a few sentences of lyric as excuse and accompaniment for the lyrical *solo* of the heroine.

There was another way, less courageous but on the whole more likely to succeed, namely to treat the chorus rigidly as a convention, to exclude it altogether from the action, though allowing it still to mark divisions between scenes. There is no reason why the choral *entr'acte* should not play upon the motives of the drama, and add to its effect, but logically the musicians should be silent except in the intervals. That is a method which Euripides, like Sophocles, sometimes tends to adopt. He does not adopt it outright, and his art suffers from a conflict between the tendency to make the chorus real and the tendency to make them conventional.

There are, of course, occasions when the lyrical form is consistent with Euripidean realism. When a company is seized by strong emotion (panic, for instance, as in the *Seven*, or enthusiasm, as in the *Bacchants*) the varied rhythms, the music and the dance are an aid, not a hindrance, to realistic expression. Now the portrayal of violent emotion was a part of the Euripidean method; and his characteristic *monodies*, lyrical *soli* sung by the actor on the stage, are in most cases used to heighten the effect of some strong feeling. The realism of Euripides is not photographic. Those who talk of his language, for instance, as if it were that of the Athenian market-place, are deceived by its art. It is not the language of common life. Nor is it, like that of Sophocles, more alive than ordinary speech. Simply it is more lucid, capable of expressing in easy polished

sentences all manner of ideas. Therefore a lyrical
monody is a not incongruous expression for the strong
emotion of characters who ordinarily talk the language
of Euripides. Examples are the tragic marriage-song
of Cassandra in the *Trojan Women*, and the splendid
outburst of Creusa in the *Ion*. The one instance of
a monody expressing "calm and gentle sentiments"
is, as M. Decharme observes, that of the young temple
servant, Ion. There the effect is natural because the
poet is creating an atmosphere of romance. The
realism of the *Ion* is in the sordid tale which is
contrasted with the beauty of the setting. The more
romantic Ion seems, the more effective is his gradual
realisation that Apollo is either a ravisher and child-
deserter, or a fraud, or an excuse for fraud, or all
these things, or nothing.

Why, it may be suggested, did not Euripides, who
had ideas to preach, find in the chorus, as Aeschylus
had found, a vehicle for his opinions? The answer
has already been implied. The ideas of Aeschylus,
though they were in advance of current notions,
were ultimately religious, tended to a harmonising
of popular belief with truth. Euripides, on the
other hand, whatever precisely he thought, held certainly opinions which he dared not generally utter
by the mouth of the religious chorus. The opinions
expressed by his chorus are as a rule conventional
and pious: sometimes irony is felt behind the

convention, and the pious moralising reveals the inadequacy of current sentiment. But for the direct expression of his own opinion Euripides could not use the chorus. His characters therefore are to some extent their own chorus. That is one reason for their loquacity. They say not simply what a man *would* say in such and such a situation, but what a man *might* say or *think*. Sometimes their speeches are dramatic: sometimes they express opinions about which we can only say that Euripides thought them interesting: occasionally we can feel sure that the opinions are the opinions of the poet: often, however, the characters, like the chorus, express the conventional view in order that it may refute itself.

The technique of Euripides is thus almost inevitably associated with his general point of view. With regard to both it must be apparent that the present writer accepts with gratitude the teaching of Dr Verrall. The lucidity of Euripides is deceptive; it is a mistake to assume that he approves of his story or his hero; he does not necessarily sympathise with the sentiments that come so glibly from the mouth of the actor. His tendency was to treat the story as a piece of ordinary life, though he was checked at every turn by convention. The result is inevitably that the legend, thus presented, is exposed. Euripides was aware of that, and was sometimes quite deliberately exposing latent immorality. Sometimes he meant

his audience to feel uneasy, to think that if the story
were true it was highly discreditable: sometimes he
meant them to infer that it was not true. But
Dr Verrall goes further. He believes that by scattered "hints and signals and cues," intelligent
Athenians, acquainted with the method, could detect
a rationalistic explanation of the myth, a theory as
to its possible origin. On that point it is well to
avoid dogma, and to generalise about Euripides is
always dangerous; but it is at least not proven that
the audience were ever intended to reflect:—"Thus
indeed, or in some such way, the thing may have
taken place, and the story may have arisen." It is
doubtful whether even in the most intelligent circles
the rationalising of miracle and the power of fallacy-
hunting were sufficiently advanced to make such a
reflection possible. In general the exposure of the
myth is moral rather than intellectual. Inconsis-
tencies are sometimes pointed out, but it is the naked
presentation of the moral grossness of the legends
which is characteristic and which must have thrilled
the audience with horror or delight. The intellectual
achievement of Euripides is this:—that a story which
is ostensibly a celebration of a god may in its
effect expose his immorality, and that a piece of
rhetoric which is ostensibly a tirade against women
may in effect expose the egoism of the man who
utters it.

I have been trying to suggest the general impression made by Euripides on his contemporaries, and the general tendency of his mind. To leave the matter there might imply that all his plays are of a like nature. The truth is, his variety of form is as great as his mental versatility. Many critics, after Aristotle, have been led astray by judging him as if he aimed at effects like those of Sophocles, but there is another habit equally misleading. I mean the habit of supposing that all his plays were meant to produce similar effects, and were constructed on similar principles. Every tragedy must be considered separately before we can see what *in each particular tragedy* Euripides was in fact attempting to do. Rules which apply, criticisms which are pertinent, to one type of drama are impertinent and misleading in regard to another.

Sometimes, to begin at the beginning, Euripides purposely and for a definite effect adopts the form of the old lyrical tragedy, the illustrating by song and speech and action of some dramatic theme or situation. In this old type there was no advancing plot, no unity of action, but, from beginning to end, simply the unity of a lyrical poem. In Euripides, when he adopts this style, dialogue occupies the greater part of the time, but the construction has all the looseness of the lyrical form. The difference between this type of drama as composed by Euripides and the earlier compositions is this, that instead of choral lyrics interspersed with dramatic tableaux we now have loosely connected dramatic scenes interspersed with choral lyrics. The finest example is the *Trojan Women*, a dramatic sequence, partly acted, partly sung, whose theme is the fall of Troy, the horror of conquest, the degradation of the conquerors, the beauty that may belong to extreme sorrow. Upon the old queen Hecuba crowd the calamities of Troy and the insolence of Greece. The whole is shot with reminiscence of the *Agamemnon*, and doubtless of lost epics, the *Sack of Troy* and the *Returns of the Heroes*. There was moreover a living meaning in this vision of the wrong which conquest entails. A few months before the performance, Melos had been punished for revolt with a cynicism which Thucydides, for all his lack of superstition, made the fatal turning point in the war. The poem is a poem, not a political tract. But the sympathy with weakness and the hatred of oppression were felt more strongly by the poet and were more moving in his drama because of things which Athenians had lately done. In its spirit and in details—the confronting of Helen with Hecuba, for instance, and the pathos given to the death of a child, Astyanax—the poem is Euripidean. In composition it is of the old free type.

Both the *Heracleidae* and the *Suppliant Women*

are performances of an old-fashioned kind on themes
of Attic glory.   In each the simple theme (a coming
of weak suppliants to Athens, a fight for their cause,
victory and the promise of benefits that piety has
earned) proves inadequate in these days when the
part of the chorus is comparatively small.   In each
the play is lengthened and the interest complicated
by an episode.   The excuse is the freedom of the
old-fashioned type of drama.   In the *Heracleidae*
soothsayers demand a human sacrifice for the success
of Athens, and Macaria, a daughter of Heracles, offers
herself as a noble victim.   Iolaus, the old comrade
of Heracles, goes to the fight, and is miraculously
re-endowed with youth.   It is true, as Dr Verrall
has pointed out, that the speaker who narrates this
incident alludes to it with a pleasant touch of scepticism.   It is true also that at the end there is a wholly
Euripidean scene, in which Alcmena stands for the old
doctrine of revenge, and Eurystheus, the traditional
villain of the piece, appeals from her murderous
clamour to the fairness of Athenian citizens.   Apart
from details, however, the piece appears to be a
frankly patriotic show, not "a satire on the barbarity
of ancient religion and manners."   In passing we may
notice that the *Hecuba*, a play of the old-fashioned
kind, since its unity depends entirely on the central
figure of the queen, suggests in more perfectly constructed drama the same moral issues which were

felt in episodes of the *Heracleidae*. The wickedness
of the religious slaughter of Polyxena recalls Macaria,
and the terrible revenge of Hecuba indicts again the
popular opinion (sanctified by proverb) that it is
right to hate an enemy and to exact full vengeance.

The *Suppliant Women* is a treatment of a theme
familiar from Chaucer, at the beginning of whose
Knight's Tale, Theseus,

> In all his wealth and in his moste pride
> He was war, as he cast his eye aside,
> Wher that ther kneled in the hye weye
> A companye of ladies, tweye and tweye,
> Ech like the other, clad in clothes blake.

These ladies are the mothers of the chieftains slain
before the walls of Thebes (cf. p. 60), and their
petition is that Athens of her piety will force the
Thebans to give up the bodies for burial. Here, as
in the *Antigone*, Creon and the Thebans violate the
sacred rights of the dead. Nor was it only in legend
that those old enemies of Athens were held guilty of
such impiety: after the battle of Delium in 424 B.C.
they refused for some time to give up Athenian dead.
Probably that fact was in the mind of the audience.
In any case the play is full of patriotic sentiment, and
for Athenians any faults of construction must have been
outweighed by the flattering piety of tone. The scene
is holy Eleusis: characteristically the poet has made
a woman of Athens intercede for the Argive mothers:

to the prayers of the women are added those of
Adrastus, leader and survivor of the expedition. The
first half is, then, a simple presentation of the petition
and its success. The latter half, however, must have
seemed most thrilling. The Athenians are victorious,
the bodies are brought to Athens, and in a solemn
ceremony they are burnt, Capaneus who died by the
lightning of Zeus on a separate pyre, the rest together.
The ceremony recalls the public funeral in which
Athenians who died in war were honoured by the
state, the occasion made memorable for us by the
Funeral Speech of Pericles: to suit this ceremony
Adrastus makes a panegyric of the dead that illustrates the freedom which such patriotic shows admit,
since his praises have no relation to the traditional
characters of the heroes, but remind us of Athenian
warriors and statesmen. In a scene of fine melodrama
Evadne, the wife of Capaneus, throws herself into the
flames of her husband's pyre; the children of the
fallen heroes bear a part in the lamentation; and, to
crown the whole, Athene herself appears. She bids
the Athenians exact from Adrastus an oath of an
abiding Argive friendship to her city (an oath which
may well be meant to be the ancient counterpart
of a modern alliance), and foretells a time when
the children shall avenge on Thebes their fathers'
wrongs.

At this point may be mentioned a curious

entertainment, composed on an original scheme, but
only to be understood if we remember the old lyrical
tradition. This is the *Phoenissae*, in which Euripides
has compressed into one play reminiscences of the
whole cycle of Theban legends. The pleasure of
witnessing this drama must have depended on a
knowledge of much literature now lost : happily we
possess enough to make most of the scenes alive.
The *Seven*, the *Antigone*, the *Oedipus Tyrannus*
and even the *Oedipus at Colonus* (which was not yet
produced, but was probably based on earlier poetry)
must be known before we can appreciate this strange
performance. The whole Theban legend in one
drama : that is the task which Euripides set himself.
And so Iocasta, the wife and mother of Oedipus, who
in Sophocles committed suicide before the self-
blinding of her husband, is here preserved alive to
speak the prologue and to kill herself over the bodies
of the sons whom she has tried to reconcile. Oedipus
also must be there ; so he is not in banishment, but
kept in the palace, a blind old man, to appear and
lament his sons in a scene which recalls his last
appearance in the *Oedipus Tyrannus*. Creon is there
and, that nothing may be wanting, he forces the blind
prophet Teiresias to reveal a fatal secret, the divine
command that he should sacrifice his son. Of course
the impious Creon refuses the sacrifice: of course,
like Haemon, the son Menoeceus seems to yield to

his father, but slays himself in spite of him. Antigone
is there, though a certain clumsiness has made critics
suspect that some of her scenes are due to changes
made at revivals. In view of the peculiar nature of
the work, the hypothesis is unnecessary. In the *finale*,
for instance, it is true that Antigone would find it
difficult to explain to a cross-examiner how she can
stay at Thebes to bury her brother and also go with
her father into exile: but the excitement of the lyrics,
and the pleasure of recognising that all the elements
of the legend have been somehow worked in, may
have prevented hearers from attempting cross-ex-
amination. As for the brothers, the poet, not content
with showing Eteocles, has contrived an interview
between them, in which, characteristically, the defender of Thebes is made odious, the returning exile
Polyneices rather attractive. Eteocles implies a
criticism of Aeschylus when he observes that it
would be waste of time to tell the names of all the
champions when the enemy is at the gates. Yet we
are not deprived of the traditional catalogue ; only,
Euripides has a new and plausible way of working
that too into his scheme ; for Antigone has surveyed
the advancing army from the ramparts, in a lyrical
scene of considerable beauty. Even now we are not
at the end of ingenuities. More than the tale of
Oedipus and his children is to be included. Laius is
brought in by the prologue, spoken by his wife, whose

elaborate detail we now can understand : she speaks also of Phoenician Cadmus, ancestor of Theban kings, by whose person Thebes is connected with the eastern world. Finally the chorus have their part in the scheme. They are Phoenician women, descended from Agenor, father of Cadmus, and so related to the Theban princes : they claim kinship with Argive Io, and are so related to the invading army. They happen to be here because war broke out when they were staying with their Theban kinsmen on their way to Delphi, where they were to be consecrated to the service of the god. Could anything be more ingenious ? They can sing of Cadmus and Harmonia and the dragon's teeth ; of Apollo whose name (as we saw in the *Seven*) stood for so much in the story ; and, with equal appropriateness, of the Sphinx and of the Erinyes that haunt the royal house. They are equally at home in prayers to Io, and to the gods of Thebes, and to the gods of Delphi. Thus their persons and their songs form a kind of cement, which binds together the different motives, and fills in the gaps in this great edifice of reminiscence. The whole is a dramatic *fantasia* of Theban legend, and cannot justly be expected to conform to the standards of an ordinary play.

But Euripides did sometimes write plays. Consider, for instance, the *Medea*, the wonderful proof that a Greek could sympathise with a woman, a bad woman, and—strangest of all—a barbarian. It is a strain upon our sympathy when Medea, having killed her children simply to hurt the man who had abandoned her, departs for Athens on her flying car. There are signs that the poet felt embarrassment, but was driven by tradition to end his tragedy so. In any case the play shocked Athenians, partly because the mere representation of so terrible a love and hate was felt to be immoral, but also, I think, because the wicked witch was treated with too great a sympathy. As for the heroic Jason, if only we will listen with our minds, we shall realise that he stands, and is meant to stand, for the eternal selfishness of men. His views of Medea, of the advantages (which she ought to appreciate) of living in a Greek city, of his princess, of women and of life, are *mutatis mutandis* the views of Sir Willoughby Patterne. Similarly in the *Hippolytus*, another drama very shocking to orthodox taste (though the form in which we have the play is said to be a second version with the impropriety toned down), we are actually made to sympathise with Phaedra, one of the Greek counterparts of Potiphar's wife, worse indeed than Potiphar's wife, since her passion was for her stepson. Euripides makes pity prevail over disapprobation; he makes us feel that Phaedra is like most of us, only more unfortunate rather than more wicked ; and he suggests reflections by the picture of the selfish vulgar nurse,

10—2

and in other ways, as to the kind of life an Athenian
lady leads, and the results which must be expected
in a woman of passionate nature. As for the virtuous
hero, he is noble, but he has a touch of priggishness.
Thus, instead of a piece of edification, we have a
tragedy of two real human beings, the one carried
away by the passion of love, and the other lacking it
altogether. Artemis and Aphrodite are accessories,
incarnations of two warring elements in man, asceti-
cism and sexual love. Probably Greek feeling saw
nothing shocking in such a conception, nor would any
Greek have been shocked (as some modern critics
are) by the powerlessness of Artemis to save her
favourite. Two points may be mentioned which may
not be detected in the reading of the drama, but are
clear enough when it is acted. The motive of Phaedra,
when she kills herself and leaves the slander that
incriminates the man she loves, is not simply the
desire to keep an honourable name. Her thought is
not merely, nor perhaps chiefly, for herself. It is the
good name of her children that she wishes to save.
That fact is perhaps less clearly emphasised because
it was so obvious to a Greek audience. For a parallel
we may go to modern Japan, where in this matter as
in regard to ancestor-worship, patriotism, filial duty,
and many other things, instinctive feeling is nearer to
the Greek than ours. It helps us to understand why
Euripides was so scandalous when he exhibited love

stories on the stage if we consider the following sentence of Lafcadio Hearn : "The typical woman often figures in Japanese romance as a heroine; as a perfect mother; as a pious daughter, willing to sacrifice all for duty ; never as a sentimental maiden, dying or making others die for love " : and again, "Our novels seem to them indecent for somewhat the same reason that the Scripture text, 'For this cause shall a man leave his father and mother, and shall cleave unto his wife,' appears to them one of the most immoral sentences ever written." A man who tried to break down all that sentiment would be thought, as was Euripides, indecent and the hater of good women.

The *Alcestis* exposes the average man's attitude to women by a different method. Here the heroine is a good woman, worshipped for her self-sacrifice, Alcestis who died for her husband. There is no irony in the treatment of her heroism, but the poet says something like this: "Yes, a good wife, whom you do well to honour. But the husband? The friend and host of Apollo? He accepted such a sacrifice, and let his wife, the mother of young children die? As for his vaunted hospitality, his welcoming of Heracles when his wife was lying dead, is that so fine? Is it not rather, perhaps, indecent?" Alcestis, though she dies for him, has in her last moments insight into his character: his protestations leave her, and the audience, cold. When she dies, it is the voice of her

child, not the voice of Admetus, that touches us.
Admetus is real, and terribly selfish : therefore to
those who thought of him as a friend of the gods,
the drama must have been disquieting. As for the
fight of Heracles with death it seems to me to have
interested Euripides very little : this, with the fact
that the *Alcestis* was an experiment, a serious drama
substituted for the satyric play, sufficiently accounts
for the incongruous traits in Heracles. The suggestion that Alcestis was not dead but simply in a trance
is not, I think, convincing.

In the plays of which we have spoken there are
hints of the attitude of Euripides towards the gods,
but they are scattered and incidental. The *Ion*, on
the contrary, which turns on the alleged birth of the
hero from Apollo and an Athenian princess, is a
barely veiled attack upon Apollo himself, or at any
rate upon Apollo as represented by piety and by the
priestly managers of his oracle. Romantic beauty,
realism, fine characterisation, and, it may be added,
wit, are combined in this masterpiece, for the exposing
of what passed for a religious story. The *Electra*,
moreover, which is from one point of view stern
realism, is also an attack on the Delphic oracle.
The murder of Clytaemnestra, which Aeschylus had
treated as a mysterious but righteous dispensation,
and Sophocles as just retribution, is regarded by
Euripides as a crime, and the guilt is put upon Apollo.

As is his habit with traditional villains, the poet makes Clytaemnestra human : she is trapped by a heartless trick, and murdered at a moment when maternal feeling has triumphed over fear. Electra illustrates

Fig. 13. The death of Neoptolemus. On the right Apollo (with his bow) sits and approves: in the background is his temple, on the left his priestess (with the key). Orestes, with drawn sword, crouches behind the omphalos; Neoptolemus, attacked on both sides, stands at bay on an *altar*. (Tripods, omphalos, sacred palm-tree are familiar objects in front of the Delphic temple.)

a favourite motive, the degrading effect of misery upon the character. The worthy peasant is a good example of the doctrine that low birth is consistent with nobility of life : even democratic Athens thought enough of birth to find that rather obvious suggestion interesting. The *Andromache,* a melodrama, full of hatred for Sparta (as represented by the lurking Menelaus), characteristically contrasts the weak, vain, jealous, superstitious Greek Hermione with the noble Trojan Andromache. There is also an implied attack on Delphi : for the plot by which Neoptolemus is murdered reflects no more credit on the ministers of Apollo than on their *protégé* Orestes.

The *Heracles* is a fine drama, but when the legend was still part of popular belief it had also the effect of a destructive criticism. The suggestion that the construction is spoilt by the double plot is due to failure to imagine the effect upon Athenians. The tendency is to show that the current myth is indefensible, or at any rate cannot be reconciled with the belief that the government of the world is good. The first part, with its picture of the family of Heracles, oppressed by the tyrant in their father's absence and delivered as if by miracle at his return, is intended to impress us with the merit of the hero. The sequel shows whether, in the words of the chorus, spoken just before Madness appears, "that which is just is pleasing to the gods."

But again Euripides wrote plays of different kinds. Not all, nor even most of his dramas are intended

primarily to expose the myth. The *Orestes* is a story
of meanness, rancour, and homicidal mania, skilfully
constructed as effective melodrama. The *Iphigeneia
in Tauris* has a spirit of adventure and the *Iphigeneia
at Aulis* a charming air of domestic realism. The
delicate and almost homely character-drawing of the
latter play, the suggestion of romance in the relations
of Achilles and the heroine, remind us that Euripides
was the precursor of the New Comedy, of the Greek
romantic novel, and, through these, of the modern
novel. The *Hypsipyle*, of which several scenes have
lately been discovered, belongs to this class of romantic
and adventurous melodrama. The *Helena* is of all
the plays the most fanciful : the touch of the poet
here is light and humorous : the incidents are ex-
quisitely unconvincing. The effect is that of a
graceful, somewhat pathetic, but only half serious
romance.

Finally in the *Bacchants*, composed in Macedonia,
Euripides has created so sympathetic a picture of
fanatical enthusiasm that some people have believed
the work a recantation. The opinion will not bear
investigation, but it is equally inaccurate to call the
play an attack on Dionysus. In Macedonia Euripides
saw the efforts of a Hellenising king to give discipline
and order to a barbarous people : he saw also the
worship of Dionysus, god of nature and intoxicated
life, in its wild state, untamed by the Hellenic

moderation. He saw the ecstasy that devotees attained, the poetical beauty, and in a sense the
goodness, of this freedom from restraint. The intole-
rance and the dangerous zeal and the contempt for
reason and good government were also obvious to the
observer who did not believe. In a tragedy (based
on a well-known legend of a king who had opposed
the young Dionysus), Euripides has presented both
sides of this matter. Pentheus is right. Law and
order are good, and ought to be maintained. Only,
if you maintain them you do it at a price. Reason is
on the side of Pentheus, yet Dionysus also is right.
Emotion is on his side. It is a case of reason against
fundamental and volcanic forces which, like reason,
are a part of human nature. The triumph of Euripides
the Rationalist is that he also understood the spirit
of Dionysus.

Of the lingering death of Attic Tragedy this is not
the place to speak. Though tragedy languished, theatres
sprang up throughout Greece, and guilds of profes-
sional actors, called " the Artists of Dionysus," acted
and prospered. From the fourth century one play
survives, the *Rhesus*, a poor composition on an
incident from Homer. But for us Greek Tragedy
is the art that was born and flourished and died
with the great Athenian democracy of the fifth
century.

NOTE

The following complete texts are the most accessible: Aeschylus, A. Sidgwick (Oxford Classical Texts); Sophocles, R. C. Jebb (Cambridge University Press); Euripides, Gilbert Murray (Oxford Classical Texts). There are literal prose translations of Aeschylus by W. G. and C. E. S. Headlam, of Sophocles by Jebb, of Euripides by E. P. Coleridge, and verse translations of Aeschylus by A. Swanwick, E. D. A. Morshead, A. S. Way (also of the *Agamemnon* by W. G. Headlam in his edition, and of the *Prometheus* by R. Whitelaw), of Sophocles by R. Whitelaw, and of Euripides by A. S. Way (also of some plays by Gilbert Murray). Verse translations should be checked by reference either to the original or to literal prose versions. Other works which will be found useful are Haigh's *Attic Theatre*, revised by Pickard-Cambridge (for Antiquities), Farnell's *Cults of the Greek States*, vol. v. (for Dionysus), Ridgeway's *Origin of Greek Tragedy* (for Hero-worship), Murray's *History of Greek Literature*, the essays on Aeschylus by J. A. Symonds (*Studies in Greek Poets*), on Sophocles by Jebb (*Essays and Lectures*) and J. W. Mackail (*Lectures on Greek Poetry*), and the works of Decharme and Verrall on Euripides.

Two works of the first importance to all serious students of Greek Tragedy have been published since this book first appeared in 1911. The first is Professor Wilamowitz-Moellendorf's text of Aeschylus, which is, I think, the best text hitherto published. The second is the edition, in three volumes, of the Fragments of Sophocles, begun by Jebb, continued by Walter Headlam, and now happily completed by Dr A. C. Pearson, with a sound judgment and an erudition which have made the book a worthy monument of Cambridge scholarship. I desire also to mention the valuable collection of the recently discovered papyrus fragments of Greek Tragedy (*Fragmenta Tragica Papyracea*, edited by Dr Hunt, Oxford Classical Texts): Professor Flickinger's work on *The Greek Theatre and its Drama*, Chicago University Press; and last, but by no means least, Professor Gilbert Murray's admirable introduction to the study of Euripides, in the Home University library.

APPENDIX

SIMPLE METRICAL PHRASES

The paper by the late Dr W. G. Headlam on "Greek Lyric Metre," *Journal of Hellenic Studies*, vol. XXII. p. 209, should be consulted. These examples and references are compiled partly from that paper and partly from papers privately printed for Dr Headlam.

(1) *Dorian phrases* as:

(1) ⌣ | ‒⌣⌣‒⌣⌣‒⌣

(2) ‒⌣‒‒

and the combination of the two:

(3) ‒⌣‒⌣‒⌣⌣‒⌣⌣

(A period may close with (1) ‒⌣‒⌣‒‒⌣‒ or (2) ‒⌣‒⌣‒‒).

Appropriate subjects: *virtue* (*And.* 761), *self-control* (*Med.* 624), *courage, Dorian Heroes*, especially *Heracles* (*Trach.* 500, *Tro.* 801), *Castor and Pollux* (*Hel.* 1496), *Greeks)(Orientals* (*Hec.* 899). This type is burlesqued in Eur. *Cycl.* 356.

(2) Take the *trochaic* phrase often used for serious passages by Aeschylus, *e.g. Ag.* 686 ‒⌣‒⌣‒⌣‒ (cf. 171), and substitute a dactyl for one of the trochees; the new phrase we may roughly class as *glyconic.*

The commonest phrases of this type are (e.g. *Cho.* 381, 411)

(1) ‒⌣‒⌣⌣‒(⌣)‒

(2) ‒⌣⌣‒⌣⌣‒⌣

A rapid and brilliant rhythm used to express various emotions, appropriate *e.g.* to Dionysus.

Divide the phrasing so that you begin with the two shorts: the effect obtained is *Anacreontic*, appropriate to wilder revelry (Eur. *Cycl.* 491), wine, love, wanton oriental grief (⌣⌣‒‒⌣‒⌣‒‒).

Another oriental, luxurious type is the *Ionic a minore* ⌣⌣‒‒⌣⌣‒‒, often combined with *Anacreontic.*

Glyconic and Ionic both used of Dionysus, *Bacch.* 64 sq.

(3) The *Paeonic* is the most subtle, varied, and moving of Greek metres: in English it has been used by Swinburne. Begin with the simplest phrase, the *cretic*: Aesch. *Sup.* 423 – ⌣ – | – ⌣ –. Now, remembering that two short syllables may take the place of one long, follow the rhythm of 435 – ⌣ – | – ⌣ ⌣ ⌣ | – ⌣ –, compare *February*, Δᾱλογενές. But the first long may be resolved into two shorts, instead of or as well as the last, and all manner of combinations are possible.

Soph. *El.* 1245 ⌣ ⌣ ⌣ ⌣ – ⌣ –, *Pers.* 641 – ⌣ ⌣ ⌣ –, February March: 645 – ⌣ ⌣ ⌣ ⌣ –, Canterbury Pilgrim: *Sup.* 550 – ⌣ ⌣ ⌣ ⌣ ⌣ –, Catharine of Arragon.

Sorrow may endure for a night, Axle of a strong king's car, Filled with the knowledge of the Lord, Trumpet upon Rhodope.

RHYTHMICAL CHANGES

Different phrases and systems are combined and interwoven. A syllable may be interposed as a *link* between two lines to carry on the movement without rest (Aesch. *Cho.* 380 Ζεῦ, Soph. *El.* 482 οὐ, Eur. *Hipp.* 754 ἤ). The end of one phrase may be repeated, *echoed*, so as to form the beginning of the next (Eur. *Sup.* 1015 ὁρῶ δὴ τελευτὰν, | ἵν' ἕστακα· τύχα δέ μοι: the syllables ⌣ – – are often so used).

Finally a phrase may be made up of two *overlapping* phrases. A simple example is the drinking song ἐν μύρτου κλαδὶ τὸ ξίφος φορήσω, made up of the two familiar rhythms – – – – ⌣ ⌣ – (glyconic) and ⌣ – ⌣ – ⌣ – – (anacreontic).

Precisely similar is *Ai.* 693. In Aesch. *P. V.* 130, the phrases combined are ≅ – ⌣ – ⌣ ⌣ – | – ⌣ ⌣ – ⌣ – – and ⌣ ⌣ – ⌣ – ⌣ – (cf. Soph. *Antig.* 781). In *Ag.* 686 sq. three phrases are combined: trochaic, anacreontic (δορίγαμβρον ἀμφινεικῆ θ'), and the phrase appropriate to *marriage*

Ὑμὴν ὦ Ὑμέναι' Ὑμήν,
Ὑμὴν Ὑμέναι' ὦ.

INDEX

Actors, 16–18

Aeschylus, life and generation, 1, 41, 55, 83, 88; created drama, 13; primarily a poet, 18, 50; his trilogies, 29, 55–6, 63–4, 68–84; effective use of old conventions, 51, 53, of traditional material, 45, 60, 72, 79, of rhetoric, 37–8, 53, 58–9, 66–7, of contrast, 57; sense of the potency of words, 36, 37, 39, 45–7, 57–9; elaboration of recurring themes, 36–7, 45–50, 52, 54, 56; his themes used by Sophocles, 99–101; his religion, 30–1, 60–4, 80; his politics, 83–4; contrasted with Sophocles, 88–9, 93, 97, with Euripides, 130, 132, 140

Agamemnon, 74–6; *Agamemnon* of Aeschylus, 73–8, 100–2, 140

Ajax, 103–4, 121

Alcestis, 149–50

Allègre, M., 104

Anaxagoras, 87–8, 122–3

Andromache, 152

Antigone, 60, 145; *Antigone* of Sophocles, 114–6, 121, 144

'Ατατή (Illusion), 48, 103

Areopagus, 71–2, 82–3

Aristophanes, 124, 127, 128–31

Aristotle, 91, 97, 114, 139

'Ατη (Distraction), 74, 78

Atossa, 1, 48–50, 54

Bacchants, 126, 135, 153–4

Burial, importance of, 60, 103, 115, 142

Burke, 96, 98

Campbell, Mr A. Y., 109

Choephoroe, 11, 78–80, 99–100

Chorus, 13, 16, 21–3, 25, 58, 96–7, 132–7, 146

Cleon, 125

Clytaemnestra, 72, 74, 76–8, 100–1, 151–2

Creon, 114–6, 142–5

Curse in family, 55–6, 59, 68–70, 73

Cyclops, 8

Dareius, 42–3, 48, 53–4

Decharme, M., 136

Deianeira, 108, 110–3

Delphi, 3, 70–1, 151

Dionysus, 3–10; his festival, 20–1; artists of, 155

Dithyramb, 7, 9–11

Dryden, 27–8

Electra, 79, 98; *Electra* of Sophocles, 99–102, 121; of Euripides, 134, 150–2

Eleusis, 80, 99, 129–30, 143

Elizabethan drama, 16, 66

Epaphus, 36, 38–9, 67

Eteocles, 56–9

Eumenides, 71, 73, 80–4, 100

Euripides, life and generation,

*Printed in Great Britain
by Turnbull & Spears, Edinburgh*